UNIVERSITY OF NORTH CAROLINA AT CHAPEL HILL
DEPARTMENT OF ROMANCE LANGUAGES

NORTH CAROLINA STUDIES
IN THE ROMANCE LANGUAGES AND LITERATURES

Founder: URBAN TIGNER HOLMES
Editor: MARÍA A. SALGADO

Distributed by:

UNIVERSITY OF NORTH CAROLINA PRESS
CHAPEL HILL
North Carolina 27515-2288
U.S.A.

NORTH CAROLINA STUDIES IN THE
ROMANCE LANGUAGES AND LITERATURES
Number 237

THE "SYNTHESIS" NOVEL
IN LATIN AMERICA

THE "SYNTHESIS" NOVEL IN LATIN AMERICA
A STUDY ON JOÃO GUIMARÃES ROSA'S *GRANDE SERTÃO: VEREDAS*

BY

EDUARDO DE FARIA COUTINHO

CHAPEL HILL

NORTH CAROLINA STUDIES IN THE ROMANCE
LANGUAGES AND LITERATURES
U.N.C. DEPARTMENT OF ROMANCE LANGUAGES

1991

Library of Congress Cataloging-in-Publication Data

Coutinho, Eduardo de Faria.
 The synthesis novel in Latin America: a study on João Guimarães Rosa's Grande sertão – veredas / by Eduardo de Faria Coutinho.
 p. – cm. – (North Carolina studies in the Romance languages and literatures; no. 237).
 Includes bibliographical references.
 ISBN 0-8078-9241-6
 1. Rosa, João Guimarães, 1908-1967. Grande sertão. 2. Latin American fiction – 20th century – History and criticism. I. Title. II. Series.

PQ9697.R76G744 1991
869.3 – dc20   91-10289
                                                                      CIP

© 1983. Eduardo de Faria Coutinho.

ISBN 0-8078-9241-6

DEPÓSITO LEGAL: V. 1.554 - 1991   I.S.B N 84-401--2064-8
ARTES GRÁFICAS SOLER, S. A. - LA OLIVERETA, 28 - 46018 VALENCIA - 1991

*To Afrânio Coutinho,
my father.*

To Malu, always.

TABLE OF CONTENTS

	Page
ACKNOWLEDGEMENTS	11
INTRODUCTION	13

PART I: LATIN AMERICAN NOVEL TODAY

1. Regionalism and Universalism 19
2. The Expansion of the Concept of Reality 27
3. The Revolution of Language 32
4. The "Synthesis" Novel 42
5. The "New Narrative" and the Medieval Romance of Chivalry .. 44
6. The Phenomenon of the "Boom" 46
7. Revitalization of the Novel Genre 49

PART II: JOÃO GUIMARÃES ROSA'S *GRANDE SERTÃO VEREDAS*

1. *Grande sertão: veredas:* a "Synthesis" Novel 53
2. Character and Space in *Grande sertão: veredas* 56
   - 2.1. The Jagunço Riobaldo 56
   - 2.2. The Sertão and the World 67
3. The Dimensions of Reality in *Grande sertão: veredas* 78
   - 3.1. The Logos and the Mythos 78
   - 3.2. The Ambiguity of Diadorim 86
   - 3.3. The Issue of Chance in Riobaldo's Life 95
4. *Grande sertão: veredas:* a Committed Novel 98
   - 4.1. The Revitalization of Language 98
   - 4.2. The Search for Expression: Living vs. Narrating 104
   - 4.3. The Monologue-Dialogue Technique 114
   - 4.4. *Grande sertão: veredas:* an Epic, Lyrical and Dramatic Work . 121

			Page
4.5.		The Real and the Imaginary in the Universe of *Grande sertão: veredas*	132
	4.5.1.	Story vs. History	132
	4.5.2.	A "Synthesis" Type of Language	137
4.6.		Guimarães Rosa's Aesthetic Revolution	141
	4.6.1.	Revitalization and Commitment	141
	4.6.2.	The Role of the Reader	147

BIBLIOGRAPHY

General Works 153
Works on Latin American Literature 157
Works by and about João Guimarães Rosa 164

ACKNOWLEDGEMENTS

I express my gratitude to Dr. Eric O. Johannesson, of the University of California – Berkeley, for his invaluable assistance during all phases of this work. My best thanks also to Dr. Benjamin M. Woodbridge, Jr., for his reading of the manuscript and his precise criticism and comments; to Dr. Jayne L. Walker, Dr. Arthur L. Askins and Dr. L. Elaine Hoover, for their careful examination of the work; to Dr. Milton M. Azevedo and Dr. Francesca von Broembsen, for their stimulating ideas and thoughful suggestions; to Dr. Fred Clark and Dr. María Salgado, of the University of North Carolina – Chapel Hill, for their encouragement to publish this work; to Dr. Eduardo Portella, Dr. Bella Jozef and Dr. Anthony Naro, of the Federal University of Rio de Janeiro, for their friendly help during my research; to my students at the Federal University of Rio de Janeiro for their interest and their feedback in class; to CAPES (Coordenação de Aperfeiçoamento de Pessoal de Nível Superior) and the Federal University of Rio de Janeiro for their financial aid during my period of residence at the University of California – Berkeley; and to Ms. Florence C. Myer for her indispensable efforts in editing and typing this text.

Finally, I thank my parents, Vanda and Afrânio Coutinho, who developed throughout my life a taste for Literature and Arts; my children, Rodrigo and Eduarda, for their always stimulating presence; and my wife, Malu, without whose love and understanding I would not have been able to accomplish this work.

E. C.

INTRODUCTION

> Macunaíma ... subiu na montaria e deu una chegadinha até a boca do rio Negro pra buscar a consciência deixada na ilha de Marapatá. Jacaré achou? nem ele. Então o herói pegou na consciência dum hispanoamericano, botou na cabeça e se deu bem da mesma forma.
>
> MÁRIO DE ANDRADE, *Macunaíma*

Literary narrative in Latin America[1] has always been characterized, throughout its historical development, by the presence of a tension between two opposing trends which are usually expressed in terms of a series of antinomic pairs such as regionalism vs. universalism, objectivism vs. subjectivism, aestheticism vs. social concern. These trends reflect on a wider level the oscillation, typical of Latin American culture, between an accommodation to the models transposed to the continent by the European colonizers and a search for national identity. In the "new narrative,"[2] they merge, nevertheless, making way for a kind of "synthesis" form

---

[1] The term "Latin American" is employed in this study not as a synonym of "Spanish American," but rather for the definite purpose of including Brazil in the panorama. However, the use of this generic term does not imply that the specific character of the literatures of both Brazil and every Spanish-speaking country of the continent is not recognized.

[2] The type of fiction referred to here is that which began to appear in the 1930's and 40's with writers such as Miguel Angel Asturias and Alejo Carpentier, in Spanish America, and Graciliano Ramos, in Brazil, and reached its climax in the 60's with the so-called phenomenon of the boom. Among the most representative authors of this kind of fiction, frequently designated by critics as "the new narrative of Latin America," are: Juan Rulfo, José Lezama Lima, João Guimarães Rosa, Julio Cortázar, Augusto Roa Bastos, José Donoso, Mario Vargas Llosa, Carlos Fuentes and Gabriel García Márquez.

that embraces in its own corpus all those traditionally opposing elements.

These trends, of course, are not restricted to Latin America – they are also present, in some of their forms, in Western literature in general – and their merging has also occurred all over the Western world during the twentieth century. However, this phenomenon assumes a special significance in the context of Latin America because it constitutes a decisive step in the long process of maturity through which fiction has gone in the continent, and marks the projection of this fiction into a universal sphere – often referred to by critics as "the boom of the Latin American novel."

The opposition between regionalism and universalism, considered in general terms, is constituted by two lines of fiction centered around two different poles – nature and man. In Latin American literature it is often confused with another opposition, of a more superficial sort, which can be identified by the terms rural vs. urban. Thus, on one side there is a "regionalist" narrative, marked by a preoccupation with describing the land, the typical rural setting, and on the other a "universalist" kind of fiction, focusing on man's psychological and existential conflicts and usually having an urban or cosmopolitan center as it setting. In the first case the emphasis is mainly the landscape, which is presented with a maximum of details, and man is relegated to a secondary level as a pure representative of the region in focus. In the second case he is the central element and the landscape a mere background very seldom characterized.

The treatment given to the elements which characterize each of these lines of fiction changed considerably within the traditional narrative – for example the portrayal of the landscape evolved from a naive, uncritical view based on merely exotic or picturesque descriptions of local color to a more critical perspective committed to exposing the social, political, or economic situation of a certain region or country. Yet, no change was sufficient to deeply affect the prevalent *status quo,* and the dichotomies between man and nature, city and countryside continued to prevail. In the example just given, the concern with the typical setting continued to be so prominent that the landscape still stood above man, and the human figure, stripped of all its complexity, maintained its role as a simple instrument or type.

In the "new narrative," however, which began in the late 1930s and early 1940s, the opposition represented by these two lines of fiction – the "regionalist" and the "universalist" – is neutralized in the context of Latin American literature. Here there occurs a shift in the "regionalist" novel's center of gravity from nature to man, and the core of this kind of fiction reveals an intricate body of human relationships. Now, man is also the pivotal element in this line of fiction, and the landscape, rather than being placed on a higher level, is seen through the human figure; in other words, it is humanized.

Yet this shift in focus within the framework of the "regionalist" narrative does not imply, as some critics have believed, an abandonment of the regional dimension, nor does it indicate that this line of fiction is supplanted by the "universalist" one. The regional elements continue to be present and alive within the "new narrative," and their importance can easily be recognized if we think, for instance, of the selection of subjects and themes and of the use of language in these works. The difference lies in the fact that now the land is no longer treated as an autonomous entity, but is inhabited by man; that is, it is presented from the perspective of the characters. In the novels and short-stories of this phase, the regional, local, or typical elements coexist side by side with the universal or generic, and this very aspect characterizes them best.

The opposition between objectivism and subjectivism, or to put it better, between objective realism and other levels of reality, is also constituted, in the context of Latin American literature, by the existence of two traditional currents of fiction – one of a romantic, idealistic sort and the other of a realistic, objective, and even pragmatic nature. These two currents, although they sometimes coincided within the same period, usually alternated with each other in the history of Latin American fiction, and the predominance of one of them at the expense of the other marked important moments in the development of this fiction. Thus the predominance of the idealistic current, first at the time of Romanticism and later at the time of Spanish-American Modernism, determined the appearance of the "Indianist" and the "Modernist" novels respectively, and the predominance of the realist current, first at the time of the Realist and Naturalist movements and then in the first two or three decades of the twentieth century, was responsible for the dominion exerced by the realist novel, especially in its so-called "socially committed" form, throughout this period.

This alternating movement resulting from the oscillation of the two opposing trends also ceases, however, in the mid-twentieth century, giving way to a sole hybrid form, based on a multiple concept of reality which embraces both the idealistic and the realistic perspectives. By this time the notion of relativity, so crucial in twentieth-century thought, has become dominant in Latin America and reality, no longer seen from a one-sided point of view, can no longer be expressed by one of those types of fiction alone. Reality is now, for the contemporary Latin American writer, something multiple and dynamic, something that has no limits and is composed of a multiplicity of levels; thus it can be represented only by means of a form that tries to apprehend it in as many of its aspects as possible. An the "new narrative," by fusing in its own corpus the two opposed perspectives embodied by the traditional trends and by adding to this fusion other elements never before given much attention in the literature of the continent — such as the mythical and magical components — fulfills this basic requisite and consequently constitutes a very suitable form to express this new world view. This narrative is a plural, global, or total form — well suited to represent the multidimensional reality of its time.

The opposition between aestheticism, or rather, aesthetic consciousness, and social concern is like the preceding ones represented by the presence of two lines of fiction centered around two distinct poles — an "aestheticist" current, based primarily on a preoccupation with form, and a "committed" current, almost exclusively concerned with the "content," which considered language as a mere vehicle for the transmission of ideas. These two lines of fiction are closely associated with two different conceptions of literature, whose one-sided perspective has frequently been questioned by criticism — the conception of art for art's sake and that which considers literature a means to achieve other aims, extraneous to the literary fact. However, they have also run alternately throughout the history of Latin American fiction and have found important expressions in forms which range from the Symbolist or Impressionist novel to the "socially committed" one.

Yet in this case as well, the two traditional trends merge in the twentieth century, giving way to a kind of narrative in which a highly committed attitude in the sociopolitical sense not only coexists with a strong preoccupation with form but also is expressed by the very form of the work, which consists of a constant process of self-questioning. Based on the belief, now dominant in this period, that it is not at all possible to separate the "content" of a literary piece from the "form" it takes, and on a wider conception of literature, according to which the work is a structure formed by the harmonious balance of its component elements but at the same time set into a dialectical relationship with the outside world, the authors of the "new narrative" engage in a desperate search for form which has often been designated by critics as a "revolution of literary language." And, by casting their questioning on reality by way of a questioning on language – on the very means to represent reality – they effect a revolution of the genre so far unprecedented in the history of Latin American literature.

This synthesis which takes place in Latin America's "new narrative" as a result of the neutralization of the oppositions just discussed is the element which confers individuality to this fiction and contributes, better than any other of its aspects, to its projection into the scope of universal literature. In replacing both the necessity to stress the typical, present in the "regionalist" novel, and the tendency to deal simply with the universal or generic, characteristic of the opposing line of fiction, with a multiple perspective – according to which these aspects are dealt with naturally from the point of view of man's experience in the world – the Latin American novel indicates that it has finally reached its maturity in the continent and has conquered a space in the realm of Western literature. In replacing both the onesided views of the "objectivist" and the "subjectivist" currents, which alternated throughout the entire history of Latin American fiction, with a "total" or "all-encompassing" perspective that includes even levels such as the mythical or the magical – so significant within the continent's cultural panorama – this narrative inscribes itself simultaneously as a typical manifestation of its century and as a cogent representative of the context from which it springs. Finally, in replacing both the purely "formalistic" concern, characteristic of certain lines of fiction and the exclusive preoccupation in denouncing the sociopolitical aspects of a specific reality, with a wider perspective in which the aesthetic and the political aspects not only coexist but are mutually interrelated, it expresses its double condition of "creation" and "representation," and acquires a place of honor among the great literary achievements of the twentieth century.

It is this "synthesis" character just presented as perhaps the most relevant trait of the Latin America's "new narrative" that will be studied in this work, first in general terms and second in a Brazilian novel which can be considered as one of the highest expressions of this type of fiction in the continent – namely, Guimarães Rosa's *Grande sertão: veredas*. The work will be divided into two sections, the first part consiting of a study of the "new narrative" of Latin America leading to its characterization as a "synthesis" narrative, the second a detailed analysis of *Grande sertão: veredas* from the point of view of this aspect.

The choice of a Brazilian novel to represent the "new narrative" in Latin America comes form the belief that the literature of Brazil and of the Spanish-speaking countries of the continent has so many common aspects and such a similar historical development that it is pertinent to speak of one general corpus, in spite of the fact that they have been written in two different languages. Yet it is important to make it clear that by including Brazilian literature in this general corpus – which the critics have already labelled as Latin American literature – we are not failing to recognize the unique features of Brazilian literature, nor are we raising any doubts as to its individuality.

The emergence in the mid-twentieth century of a new type of narrative that fuses in its own body all those traditional trends of fiction which existed in Latin America is a phenomenon common to both Brazilian and Spanish American literature; thus the particular aspects of each of these literatures, however important they may be, will be considered here only when they are deemed indispensable for the understanding of this phenomenon. Brazilian literature, as well as that of the several Spanish American countries, will be approached in this study as a kind of microcosm inserted into a macrocosm – the literature of the continent as a whole, the totality of which will mostly concern us here.

Part I

THE LATIN AMERICAN NOVEL TODAY

> Artistically ineffective works are always inefficient, no matter how advanced they may be on the political level.
>
> Mao Tse-tung, *Œuvres choisies*

> How do others see us if not as a character from a novel?
>
> Philippe Sollers, *Logiques*

1. Regionalism and Universalism

There seems to be a general consensus among contemporary critics that the Latin American narrative has undergone, throughout the last four of five decades, a considerable transformation in technique and aesthetic-literary purposes and has acquired a universal projection often referred to as "the boom of the Latin American novel."

This transformation, which constitutes a decisive step in the long process of consciousness awakening and search for identity that characterizes Latin American literature, consists primarily of a shift in the novel's center of gravity from nature to man or, in other words, from a regionalist to a universal perspective.

In the years around 1930, fictionists in Latin America were so much concerned with reproducing a specific landscape that man simply appeared as a part of this landscape and was thus defined only in terms of his external aspects. The focus in their works fell entirely upon the issue of documenting in as objective a manner as possible a certain region or country, usually for the purpose of exposing its social, political, or economic context, and man's role in this realm did not go beyond that of a mere instrument. He was reduced to an archetype or a symbol, measured by labels; he was not a complex character.

The mimetic preoccupation that saturated the minds of most Latin American writers from the group of the Mexican Revolution to people like Rivera, Güiraldes, Gallegos, and Ciro Alegría, not to mention some of the figures of the "Northeastern group" in Brazil, was recognized as a representation, in Vargas Llosa's words, of "una toma de conciencia de la realidad propia, una voluntad de reivindicar a las culturas indígenas y mestizas y de encontrar, a través de ellas, una identidad nacional, en algunos casos un despertar político en torno a los problemas sociales del continente, como el feudalismo agrario, el egoísmo de las castas oligárquicas, y la penetración imperialista."[1] However, both this tapping of the consciousness of an autochthonous reality and the political awareness of the problems of the continent were expressed in a static, descriptive way, from an external perspective, similar to that employed by the late-ninetheenth-century Naturalist writers. The outer aspects which characterized the region in focus were described with a maximum of detail, and man was relegated to a secondary level as the embodiment of such aspects. He was the *gaucho*, the *llanero*, the representative of an Indian community, or the *sertanejo*, but in none of these instances was he presented or dealt with as a complex human being whose problems, though intrinsically related to the position he occupied in society, were also those of an individual as such and in his relationship to his milieu.

The shift from this descriptivistic, Naturalistic perspective to a more dynamic and wide-open one in which the center of the narrative is occupied by an elaborated body of human relationships and the human condition is portrayed with all its complexity and contradictions, freed from the tyranny of landscape, begins to occur during the thirties and forties in works like those of Graciliano Ramos in Brazil or Miguel Angel Asturias in Guatemala. But it fully takes hold only after the Second World War, at a time when

---

[1] Mario Vargas Llosa, "En torno a la nueva novela latinoamericana," *Revista de la Facultad de Humanidades* [de la Universidad de Puerto Rico, Rio Piedras], No. 1 (Sept. 1972), p. 130.

the Latin American continent as a whole seems to have found its identity by becoming aware of its underdevelopment and its role in the history of the Western world.

In an essay entitled "Literatura e subdesenvolvimiento," the Brazilian critic Antônio Cândido affirms that regionalism, as a form of underdevelopment, was and still is a stimulating force in Latin American literature.[2] His analysis of the phenomenon of regionalism in Latin American literature concludes that it has traversed three distinct stages, each characterized by a different attitude on the part of the writer toward the reality which surrounds him.

The first stage corresponds to the writer's discovery or recognition of his country's reality and finds its literary expression in the portrayal of local color and the exaltation of nature. Here, the landscape is approached from an external, superficial perspective as something exotic or picturesque and is seen almost exclusively in its positive aspects; the writer's preoccupation consists basically in incorporating such a landscape into the realm of fiction and consequently of exalting his country, by calling attention to the wealth of its potentialities. This uncritical view, based on a strong patriotic optimism, was the dominant one throughout the nineteenth century, especially after Romanticism (the Indianist movement is a clear example of this attitude) and is still found in the first decades of this century in works like those of the Brazilian storytellers Afonso Arinos, Waldomiro Silveira, and Simões Lopes Neto, to mention just a few; in Argentine writers of the "gaucho" cycle, such as Güiraldes himself; and even in some of the widely known novels of the following phase, such as Gallegos' *Doña Bárbara* and Rivera's *La vorágine*.

In the second stage of regionalism through which Latin American literature has passed – a phase that, though it began long before, reached its highest expression in the fiction produced around 1930 – the exaltation of nature gave way to a more critical depiction of reality and patriotic optimism was replaced by a kind of pessimism toward the present which revealed, as we have seen

---

[2] Antônio Cândido, "Literatura e subdesenvolvimento," *Argumento* [Rio de Janeiro], 1 (Oct. 1973), 6-24. This article was also published in *América Latina en su literatura*, ed. César Fernández Moreno, 5th ed. (México: Siglo XXI, 1978), pp. 335-44.

through the words of Vargas Llosa, some of the essential political problems of the continent. However, since the dominant tone here was that of denunciation and the main objective of this fiction was to serve an extraliterary purpose – that of influencing the public with the hope for a change in the present state of things – the landscape continued to occupy the focal plane and man's problems were limited to the specific position he held within the scope of the region represented. This second phase constitutes a step forward in Latin American literature's process of search for autonomy in the sense that the writer has evolved from a naive to a critical, committed view of the reality around him, but the attitude which lies behind it does not point to any really significant change. In both cases, a need for national affirmation is made evident by means of the emphasis given to the landscape which, through either exaltation of its picturesque aspects or criticism of its socioeconomic structure, is placed at the core of the narrative universe. There is not yet in this period a consciousness on the part of the writers of the condition of underdevelopment which characterizes their countries, although this stage does not seem far from being attained.

This consciousness is the very element which defines the third and last stage of regionalism pointed out by Antônio Cândido. Here the writer, aware of the peripheral character of his country's reality and of his own condition of Third World man, no longer sees his land as a special, isolated case but rather as a part of a wider universe in which it has an important function. At this stage Latin America is no longer an undiscovered region that has to be made known to the rest of the world by means of depiction in literary works. This job has already been performed by the previous generations; by this time the continent has a literary tradition. And the writer, having realized this fact, no longer depicts his land in its specific, typical elements alone but also in those aspects which it shares in common with the rest of the world. What matters now for the Latin American writer is not the region or country per se, as an autonomous entity, but land as it is seen through the life experience of its inhabitants. Thus the axis of this fiction comes to be occupied by man, who – from a mere slave of his own geography, from a mere patient of history – is turned into the main and perhaps sole focus of interest.

This shift of emphasis from nature to man does not imply, as it might seem at first glance, that man has come to be treated in isolation from his own environment, as one enclosed in a kind of ivory tower, or – even less – that the landscape has disappeared from the pages of the novels. On the contrary, the former has never been more involved with his environment nor has the latter been more present than it is now. The difference lies in the fact that man has become the pivotal element and the landscape, rather than ranging itself above him, has come to be seen *through* the human being – in other words, has been humanized.

The immediate consequence of this humanization of the landscape is the emergence of a new kind of hero, endowed with a much wider dimension, who – without losing track of his condition as a type, representative of a certain region – transcends this very condition and imposes himself by means of his individual action. This new hero is a complex, multidimensional being, in whose person such previously existing oppositions as that between man and nature which made, for example, the fortune of the novel of the "jungle cycle," are neutralized. Here, man and nature are no longer two separate entities frequently set into conflict, but rather the two sides of an integral totality which complement each other. The region is present in man, who reflects it in the way he relates to the world. It is alive within man, to such an extent that it is reflected in his every action, in his own way of being, but it never goes so far as to determine the scope of his actions. This deterministic perspective, responsible for the one-sided quality or condition around which the heroes of the previous novels were constucted – that is, their embodiment of the condition of specific types alone – no longer has any place in this fiction. The new hero continues to be a type in the sense mentioned that he expresses his collective character – his region or society and the function he has in that structure – in every act, but he is above all an individual whose circle of action cannot be restricted to such a space. The will which commands this hero is his own individual will, an the problems he comes across, though a reflex of his collective traits, are his own individual problems, resulting from his personal experience in the world.

This new hero, who embraces the conditions of both type and individual, and whose typically is revealed through his own individuality, can be well exemplified if we think of Guimarães

Rosa's *jagunço* Riobaldo as opposed to the *jagunço* type so frequent in earlier Brazilian regionalist fiction. Whereas the latter is a mere type that can be defined by a series of clichés which conform to an abstract, a priori model – the conception of the *jagunço* among the Brazilian literary intelligentsia – Riobaldo, the protagonist of *Grande sertão: veredas*, is the embodiment of a type representative of his region, the Brazilian backlands, but his scope as a narrative hero is not limited to such an aspect. He is, in addition to this, an individual character, a hero who transcends his typicality by means of the human dimension with which he is endowed. Riobaldo's conflicts in the universe of *Grande sertão: veredas* undoubtedly reflect all the problems characteristic of the *jagunço* type (a point which can be made clear if we compare him, for example, to the other *jagunços* in the novel), but they are at the same time individual conflicts, pertinent above all to his own existential condition. Thus one of the major concerns he has in the long life-journey he accomplishes in the novel in the question of the essence of good and evil, a matter that, while very much alive within the jagunço's world, is above all a human, existential preoccupation. Besides, although a jagunço, Riobaldo is always questioning his condition as such and the very condition of being a jagunço, which by placing a critical distance between himself as a character and the type he embodies reinforces his quality of transcending the model, and accounts for his projection into a more nearly universal realm.

Another consequence of this phenomenon of humanization of the landscape is the universalization of the region – the breaking with its strict limits and its inclusion into a wider, universal context. Since man is now the focal element in fiction and the landscape something that is basicallly seen through him, rather than in and by itself alone, it can no longer be simply presented in terms of a series of specific elements that constitute its uniqueness and are therefore considered typical. These elements are usually the clichés, the external side of things, the apparent, which have been crystallized through the years. They are merely one side of the landscape – the obvious, not its totality as they have been frequently understood. And landscape, as well as man, is a wider reality that cannot have its range reduced to such labels. In the same way that man can be satisfactorily portrayed only when seen in his complexity and contradictoriness, so the former can be fully represented only when captured in its multifaceted aspects.

Thus the landscape we encounter in the pages of such novels as *Grande sertão: veredas,* to continue with the same example, is not the accurate description of a physical reality alone – the world of the state of Minas Gerais – but rather the re-creation in as complete a manner as possible of a wider reality that has no external boundaries. The *sertão* in *Grande sertão: veredas* is certainly a faithful literary re-creation of a specific area of the Brazilian backlands, as one can tell, for example, from the abundance of precise geographical references, but more than that it is the representation of a region present and alive within the mind of the narrator-protagonist, a human, universal region that can by no means be clearly delimited. Hence Riobaldo's preoccupation, throughout the entire novel, with defining it and his inability to come up with a satisfactory conclusion. *Grande sertão: veredas* contains a large number of definitions for the *sertão,* or rather of attempts to define it, and not a single one can stand by itself. Instead, they complement and even contradict one another and are meant to make sense only when seen from this complex and global perspective: "O sertão é e não é," says Riobaldo repeatedly, "o sertão está em toda a parte" ("The sertão is and is not, the sertão is everywhere").[3]

This universalization of the region which is found in *Grande sertão: veredas,* as well as in other influential novels of this period, such as Juan Rulfo's *Pedro Páramo,* García Márquez's *Cien años de soledad,* and Vargas Llosa's *La casa verde,* indicates the weakening of the old dichotomy between rural and urban, or regional and universal, that has for so long held a place in the history of Latin American fiction. Nowadays, says Luis Harss in the study *Into the Mainstream,* "it is increasingly meaningless to distinguish between the regional and the urban. Before, the two words denoted differences of mentality; the regional was parochial: it dealt with local human types and topical problems. The urban was more complex, worldly, and therefore universal. Now the difference is becoming merely a matter of setting."[4] Some critics have tended to see this difference as the decadence or even disappearance of the regionalist novel and talk about the passage from the regional,

---

[3] João Guimarães Rosa, *Grande sertão: veredas,* 2nd ed. ["texto definitivo"] (Rio de Janeiro: José Olympio, 1958). Cited henceforth as *GS:V;* page citations will be given in the text in parentheses.

[4] Luis Harss and Barbara Dohmann, *Into the Mainstream: Conversations with Latin American Writers* (New York: Harper & Row, 1967), p. 23.

which they identify with rural, to the urban or universal. Indeed, this passage has occurred in great part as a reflex of the exodus to the cities that has marked Latin American life in the twentieth century; however, to state that the regional dimension is abandoned or overcome is surely an unjustified extrapolation. The region continues to be present and alive in this recent fiction and not exclusively as the setting for events; it is an especially important element in the selection of subjects and themes and in the elaboration of language itself. The Indian, the *llano*, the *caudillismo*, the *sertão* continue to have an active, fundamental role in Latin American fiction, and it could not be otherwise, owing to the continent's economic reality of underdevelopment. What happens is that those strata are no longer the axis or essence of fiction but rather complementary elements. As the critic Zunilda Gertel says in the preface to her *La novela hispanoamericana contemporánea*,

> Paralelamente a las novelas que tienen como realidad ambiental la vida en las ciudades, *Rayuela, Sobre héroes y tumbas, La vida breve, La ciudad y los perros, El banquete de Severo Arcángelo, La región más transparente*, podemos citar en contrapunto a *Pedro Páramo, Los pasos perdidos, Los ríos profundos, Hijo de hombre, La casa verde, Paradiso, Cien años de soledad*, donde la realidad de la naturaleza persiste con todo su primitivo poder y es evidente la constancia de la materia tradicional. La diferencia está en que esos estratos especiales de la nueva novela no tipifican, no destruyen lo individual del hombre, cuya realidad interior descubre en lo absurdo y caótico de esos mundos una misteriosa esencialidad que opera como fuerza catártica.[5]

Moreover, the fact that there has been a growing incidence of novels in which the urban, cosmopolitan element is made predominant does not at all imply the elimination of the regional dimension, but rather simply of the traditional concept of regionalism present in the two stages previously discussed – the exotic and the social. *Rayuela, Sobre héroes y tumbas,* and *La ciudad y los perros* are no less regionalist novels than *Los pasos perdidos, La casa verde,* and *Cien años de soledad* for the simple reason that they do not take place in a rural area and are dominantly centered around

---

[5] Zunilda Gertel, *La novela hispanoamericana contemporánea* (Buenos Aires: Nuevos Esquemas, 1970), p. 12.

universal preoccupations. In all these cases the regional, local, or typical elements coexist side by side with the universal or generic and are by no means less significant. It is not by denying its regional character that Latin American literature has attained its present condition of universality; on the contrary, by accepting such a character, by assuming its regional identity, it has reached its maturity and entered the realm of universal literature. The "new narrative" of Latin America is a "regionalist-universalist" fiction, and it is precisely this synthesis, this paradoxical quality which best defines it.

2. THE EXPANSION OF THE CONCEPT OF REALITY

Another fundamental aspect of the transformation that Latin American fiction has undergone in the last few decades, an aspect that reaffirms its "synthesis" character, is its expansion of the concept of reality. Although it can be said that the fiction of Latin America has a great realistic tradition, present for example in the picaresque novel, with its roots in Iberian literature,[6] the kind of realism that pervades in such fiction is definitely not the "realism of facts" that found so firm a ground in the nineteenth century. However, it is this latter kind of realism which, owing to the influence exercised by European, particularly French, culture and the role played by scientific, rationalist thought in the entire Western world in the second half of the nineteenth century, dominated the Latin American literary scene, first at the time of the Realist and Naturalist movements and then, in its socially committed form, during the first two or three decades of the twentieth century.

The first manifestation of this scientific kind of realism – the Realist and Naturalist movements – did not have a long duration in Latin America, having been quickly overtaken by Modernism in the Spanish-speaking countries and by Symbolism in Brazil, but its second manifestation – the socially committed current – went through the Vanguard movements and founded a solid tradition

---

[6] It is worth recalling here as examples the *Periquillo Sarniento*, by José Joaquín Fernández de Lizardi, in Spanish America, and *Memórias de um sargento de milícias*, by Manuel Antônio de Almeida, in Brazil.

which had its highest expression in the novel of the Mexican Revolution, the "indigenist" novel, and the Northeastern novel of the 1930's in Brazil.

Although this sociological current differs in certain aspects from the Realist and the Naturalist, the world view predominant here maintains the same absolutist perspective of the former movements – the conviction that the only true reality is the external, the objective, which is now even further reduced almost exclusively to one of its aspects, the socioeconomic – and shares the same belief that the function of literature is the faithful reproduction of such a reality. What mattered for the novelists of this period was the portrayal of the frightful, unjust reality of Latin America, especially in what concerns the social condition of the peasantry, and everything that might cross the barriers of such a reality was considered if not "unreal" as pertaining to inferior realities, and was dismissed from literature.

This one-sided, dogmatic concept of reality, together with the presupposition that literature must reproduce reality at any cost, though questioned before to some extent, falls into general discredit only when the fiction of the continent begins to switch its focus from nature to man and to transcend its regional and national bounds to enter the realm of universal literature. By this time the notion of relativity, so prominent in twentieth-century thought, seems to have become dominant in Latin America, and reality, no longer seen as the phenomenon alone, is now conceived as something multiple and dynamic, which includes other levels impossible to perceive by mere empiricism. Reality is now, for the Latin American writer, something that has no limits, that can by no means be fully defined; hence, any attempt to reproduce it faithfully is considered fallacious.

The awareness on the part of the writers of the impossibility of reproducing reality through literature has created a new mentality in Latin America, according to which the work of art has its own reality that cannot be subordinated to the reality of the outside world. The aesthetic object is, for the writers of this period, a totality formed by the harmonious balance of the various elements which compose it; thus, in order for it to be "real" every one of these elements must be coherently related to the others to produce a harmony perceived in the apprehension of the whole. The idea of Realism in art, and in literature in particular, is now based on a criterion of validity and meaningfulness – in other words, coherence – and not on the degree of fidelity which the work presents in its relation to the outside world. The literary work is not a simple imitation, a direct enunciation of this world's reality, but a representation, a transposition of such a reality into a structure that has its own rules; thus it cannot be conceived or constructed with mimetic biases. It is a human creation, an invention, and as such it can be fully realized only when approached from this perspective.

The conception of the literary work as a fictional creation does not imply, nevertheless, that it is an alien, isolated phenomenon which exists in a void. This view – of which the French Symbolist movement, especially in its late, decadent phase, and some of the European currents of the twentieth century have been accused – cannot be imputed to the "new narrative" of Latin America, where there seems always to have existed an awareness of the fact that the work both reflects and expresses the world in which it was created. For the authors of this type of narrative, the work exists in a context, the world of its author, and it cannot disregard such a context. On the contrary, it offers a view of this world and can be said to constitute an attempt to capture its essence. In other words, the work transcends itself and establishes a dialectical relationship with the world of its author.

For the authors of Latin America's "new narrative," if the literary work, though not subordinated to the external world, is also an expression, or rather a representation, of this world in an effort to penetrate its essence, and the reality of such a world is dynamic and composed of a multiplicity of levels, the work should strive to represent this reality on as many levels as possible and will thereby acquire the form of a prism or a kaleidoscope. That which was seen as reality by the previous generations is now revealed as a mere fragment of it, so that, as Vargas Llosa says, "that's the obligation of the writer who wants to be a realist [and every good writer should, according to him, attempt to be one]: to use all the means at his disposal to keep reality from dying on the operating table."[7] The highest mission of literature, for Vargas

---

[7] This and the following affirmations made by Vargas Llosa are found in Harss and Dohmann, pp. 358-60.

Llosa, is to offer man the possibility of knowing through a full grasp of all circumstances that surround him; literature is, he says, "an extraordinary instrument of knowledge," thus "the best novels are always those that exhaust their material, that don't throw a single light at reality but many. The points of view that can be brought to bear on reality are infinite," he continues, and "a novel will be greater and vaster in proportion to the number of levels of reality it presents." This novel is what Vargas Llosa calls the "all-encompassing" novel, one "that aspires to embrace reality in all its facets, in all its manifestations." He is conscious of the fact that this novel can never fulfill itself at all levels, but insists that "the greater its diversity, the broader the vision of reality, the more complete the novel will be."

A fine example of the "all-encompassing" novel for Vargas Llosa is García Márquez's *Cien años de soledad*. Here reality is represented on a wide number of levels: the historical, the objective report of everyday life, the mythical, the magical, the oneiric, the marvelous, the fantastic, or the purely imaginary. The levels all coexist and interpenetrate one another in the universe which the narrator intends to offer – the physical and mental complex of the people of Macondo, a fictitious representation of a small Latin American community; therefore they are put together in the ordinary narrative sequence and recounted with varied "simultaneity" devices which suggest their interpenetration. Thus a historical episode is narrated side by side with a mythical event, and a magical or fantastical episode is inserted in the middle of the report of a series of everyday life occurrences. But the episodes are never merely historical, mythical, or magical in Macondo – these categories of the "real" do not exist as separate entities in that world; they are narrated from a multiple, or at least a double, perspective which questions the very categories according to which they would traditionally be classified: a historical episode is frequently narrated as something symbolical or imaginary and the magical or fantastical events as natural facts that cause no surprise to the characters who experience them. García Márquez, in his discourse, not only includes various levels of reality present in the world he wants to represent but also questions their independence and consequently denounces any view of reality which is limited to a one-sided perspective.

This view of reality as multiple and dynamic and its consequent representation in literature from a multiple perspective has also another aspect which must be mentioned here – the fact that it is in much greater accord than any previous view with the spirit of Latin American people and their cultural tradition. Latin America is a land of extreme contrasts, a place where various races and cultures at different stages of development, different ages, exist simultaneously. It is the only continent, says Alejo Carpentier, in his interview with Luis Harss, "where a twentieth-century man can shake hands with a man from an age before railroads and newspapers, coexist with the Middle Ages, or be the contemporary of some other man in an isolated province who is living the Romanticism of 1850" (Harss & Dohmann, p. 43). Such a land, characterized by ambiguity, in which demographic, political, sociological, and economic extremes coexist in constant tension, can never be conceived exclusively in terms of objective realism, nor can it ever be approached or captured by means of rational devices alone.

The marvelous, the mythical, the fantastic, the other levels of reality which transcend scientific objectivity, are an integral part of Latin American life; they are present in the everyday life of the continent in its most trivial occurrences. Thus they cannot, the authors of the "new narrative" believe, be absent from its literature. "Lo real maravilloso se encuentra a cada paso en las vidas de hombres que inscribieron fechas en la historia del Continente y dejaron apellidos aún llevados," says Carpentier, in the prologue to *El reino de este mundo*, a text considered as a kind of manifest of "magic realism" in Latin American literature; and immediately afterwards, he sets the question: ". . . qué es la historia de América toda sino una crónica de lo real-maravilloso?"[8] In Latin America everything is possible, everything is real, García Márquez states, corroborating this idea, and adds that we live surrounded by all these extraordinary and fantastic events, and that yet our writers insist on telling us about "realidades inmediatas sin ninguna importancia."[9] These

---

[8] Alejo Carpentier, *El reino de este mundo* (Santiago, Chile: Editorial ORBE, 1972), pp. 11-12, 14.
[9] Gabriel García Márquez and Mario Vargas Llosa, *La novela en América Latina: Diálogo* (Lima: Carlos Milla Batres and Universidad Nacional de Ingeniería, 1968), p. 20.

extraordinary events occur every day in Latin America and our writers, rather than accepting them as reality, keep providing their readers with a series of rationalistic explanations or justifications which falsify their true nature. García Márquez criticizes this attitude still present in Latin American literature and affirms that the writer must accept his reality and include it unmasked in his books. If the cultural reality of Latin America is magical or fantastical, it has to be represented as such in the novels and short-stories. And the role of the conscious contemporary fictionist is to work in the investigation of the language and the technical forms of narrative, "a fin de que toda la fantástica realidad latinoamericana forme parte de nuestros libros y que la literatura latinoamericana corresponda en realidad a la vida latinoamericana donde suceden las cosas más extraordinarias todos los días" (ibid.). For him, it is only by accepting his "fanciful" reality and representing it in his fiction that the Latin American writer will achieve an authentic literary expression and offer a new and significant contribution to universal literature.

3. THE REVOLUTION OF LANGUAGE

The concern expressed by the writers of Latin America's "new narrative" about representing in their fiction the multidimensional reality of our time, including its magical, mythical, or fantastical levels so significant within the context of their continent, has had an important consequence which constitutes perhaps the most relevant trait of the present stage of this literature – the search for a new language for literary expression or, to use the words of the critic Rodríguez Monegal, a revolution in language.[10]

The type of language predominantly employed in the Latin American fiction of the 1920's and 30's was a descriptive one, crystallized in stereotyped formulas, which did not go beyond appearance and the conventional. It was a type of language based on clichés, on a "ready-made" view of the world, fit to represent the scientific objectivity which the advocates of the "roman á

---

[10] Emir Rodríguez Monegal, "Una escritura revolucionaria," *Revista Iberoamericana*, 37 (July-Dec. 1971), 505.

thèse" aimed to propagate. This language "llenaba su función en cuanto re-edificaba en la obra literaria un mundo que se ofrecía con formas típicas, de significación concreta inmediata y de duración previsible," as Fernando Alegría affirms in his *Literatura y revolución*.[11] But when it is used to represent the world view of the writers of the "new narrative," it is revealed as sterile and insufficient. A static world measurable by rational categories could possibly be expressed by this frozen kind of language, but not a reality that is multiple and constantly changing. Reality for the authors of the "new narrative" is something illogical, something which transcends the barriers imposed by Western logic; so, if the writer wishes to represent it in his fiction, he must liberate himself from the tyranny of such language.

This language, pretentiously objective but at the same time paradoxically rhetorical in the sense that it often wandered into long eloquent descriptions, especially in the Regionalist novel, was incapable of representing any unepidermic stratum of reality because its forms were worn out by a stagnated view of the world: words had lost their primitive energy and acquired new fixed meanings associated with one specific context (e.g. the words *selva, montaña, pampa, sertão* in the Regionalist novel); expressions had become vague and weakened, disguised with different connotations which concealed their original strength; syntax had abandoned its infinite potentialities and had limited itself to ready-made sentences and clichés. The poetic character of language, in other words, which consists exactly in its power to reveal new things, was smothered by the conventional, and hidden behind labels and stereotypes.

Aware of this process of exhaustion through which poetic language had gone and of its inadequacy to represent authentically their wiew of the world, the authors of Latin America's "new narrative" set themselves a new task – that of revitalizing their language, of making it recover its original strength. And they started by declaring war on the established forms of language, by setting fire to them, as Julio Cortázar affirms in his novel or "antinovel" *Rayuela*, a great radical example of revitalization of

---

[11] Fernando Alegría, *Literatura y revolución* (Mexico: Fondo de Cultura Económica, 1971), p. 19.

literary language. It was necessary, he says, to divest language of all its *ropa ajena,* its alien, inexpressive forms, worn out after long usage, and to search back for the primitive meaning of words, the only one close to the immediacy of things; it was necessary "terminar con la impureza de los compuestos y devolver sus derechos al sodio, al magnesio, al carbono químicamente puros."[12] Only then would words reveal themselves again in their primitive state, with all their potentialities, as natural resources yet unexploited; only then would language resume its poetic function of revelation. The writers of the "new narrative" made use of a number of procedures in order to have their language attain this stage and thus be able to express in a fresh and vivid manner the reality of their time. In other words, they made their language regain its creative character, which had for so long lain dormant behind the referent, and by so doing they recovered, as the critic Bella Jozef affirms, "o sentido criador da linguagem, as possibilidades mágicas da palavra, assimilando o fato novelesco ao poético e regressando às raízes poéticas da literatura. A imaginação se põe a serviço de uma captação da realidade, mais rica e mais complexa do que a puramente descritiva."[13]

But this process of revitalization achieved by the writers just mentioned was not limited to the various aspects of language, understood in the strict sense of a physical, acoustic entity and its written counterpart. Language also includes discourse, or rather the structure of a narrative piece: the syntax, lexicon, and morphology of a novel or a short story. In the same way that the language of a narrative work should be revitalized to express the multiple and constantly changing nature of the world, the structure of such a work had also to transcend the traditional concepts of its literary genre (such as the notions of story and plot based respectively on a chronological and causal relationship between facts) and search for new technical devices more adequate to express the multifaceted reality of its time. The authors of Latin America's "new narrative" realized this necessity and undertook a concerned search for new artifices in their craft that advanced fiction a decisive step in its history and restarted its pulse after a long period of dormancy. As

---

[12] Julio Cortázar, *Rayuela* (1963; rpt. Buenos Aires: Editorial Sudamericana, 1970), p. 488.
[13] Bella Jozef, *O espaço reconquistado* (Petrópolis: Vozes, 1974), p. 22.

a result they did what Luis Harss observed in relation to the American writers Faulkner, Stein, Hemingway, and Sherwood Anderson: "They taught the novel to talk, to find its voice and become expressive" (Herss & Dohmann, p. 30).

This necessity to revitalize the language and structure of narrative which has taken the shape of an intense search for form reveals a consciousness on the part of these writers of the role of language in a literary composition. A literary work is not content alone, say the writers of the "new narrative," but language as well; the latter is its body, an integral part of its being, thus it can never be simply a means, a mere vehicle. A literary work is created in language, so that the scope of language in literature can never be restricted to its referential aspect; on the contrary, it is exactly its capacity for transcending this aspect that makes of it the object of literature. The Latin American prose-writers of the 20's and 30's were so much preoccupied with the reality expressed that they failed to realize this fact, nowadays practically recognized as a truism, and paid no tribute to the creative function of language. Their purpose was to present a reality, especially in its negative aspects, in order to have it transformed, and they limited themselves predominantly to descriptions. It was only with the "new narrative" that the poetic function of language was fully reinstated in Latin American fiction and an effective link established between the reality expressed and the way to express it. Critic Nelson Osorio illustrates this contrast between the two generations of writers when he states that in contemporary fiction

> Ya no se trata de describir, mostrar, reflejar por medio de la palabra una realidad con la cual se tiene una relación más o menos clara y coherente —sea de aceptación o de rechazo—, sino de introducirse en ella, con un instrumento que se va forjando en el trabajo, con el arma de un lenguaje poético que va surgiendo de las necesidades de esta acción, no... para "mostrarnos" una realidad que el escritor ve y conoce, sino para tratar de situarla, de establecerla, de instaurarla.[14]

---

[14] Nelson Osorio, "Problemas del lenguaje y la realidad en la nueva narrativa hispanoamericana," *Problemas de Literatura* 1 (Jan. 1972), 41.

By saying that in Latin America's "new narrative," the writer's preoccupation is to "situate," "establish," or "restore" the desired reality "con el arma de un lenguaje poético que va surgiendo de las necesidades de esta acción," Osorio clearly defines the position assumed by the authors in relation to their language. For them, the language of a literary work is not something that preexists its construction; rather, it is a part of this work, a creation, and as such it is invented only at the moment in which the artist is giving birth to his work. The language in which a work is built up is inseparable from the material to which it is giving form; thus it is a basic condition for the writer to search for the language appropriate to his world view. Hence García Márquez says in his long and revealing conversation with Vargas Llosa at the Universidad Nacional de Ingeniería in Lima that each theme calls for the type of language best suited to express it and that such language must be sought. Asked about the reason for the difference between the language of *Cien años de soledad* and that of his other books, except *La hojarasca*, García Márquez states that the theme of that novel is entirely different and that the material he was dealing with in *Cien años de soledad* required a distinct language. And he continues: "Si mañana yo encuentro otro argumento que necesita un lenguaje diferente, trabajaré para encontrar ese lenguaje, el que más le convenga para que sea más eficaz el relato" (*La novela*, p. 49).

The conviction expressed by García Márquez and shared by all his colleagues that the problem of literature is words and that the writer has to struggle for the right form in order to create his world is, according to Vargas Llosa, the central, unifying element which characterizes Latin America's "new narrative" – an awareness of form, an artistic impulse. The novelist of this period believes that the novel is language and that his success or failure depends on the form which materializes the themes he chooses or the emotions or obsessions he expresses; therefore he commits himself entirely to the elaboration of such a form and takes his task so seriously that frequently, as is the case with *Rayuela*, the form of the novel becomes also what used to be called its content. Owing to this preoccupation with the right, exact form, García Márquez not only spent many long years, as he declares, composing *Cien años de soledad* but also had to produce four other books to learn how to write that one,[15] and authors like Guimarães Rosa and

Vargas Llosa, to continue with only a few examples, introduced so many innovations in their texts (the former mainly in terms of language *stricto sensu* and the latter in terms of structure) that narrative attained with them a stage of development hitherto unprecedented in the continent's letters.

But this investigative aspect, this intrinsic need of experimentation, prominent in the "new narrative" in Latin America, has often been misunderstood by a certain kind of criticism, from both the continent and abroad, that considers this formal preoccupation excessive and accuses the authors of being "language adventurers" who alienate themselves from their readers by pure verbal ludism. These accusations have constituted a point of departure for a series of polemics or metalinguistic essays in which the authors presented and defended their own concept of the novel, forming thus a kind of "poetics," however heterogeneous, of the new genre. But such criticism originated from a superficial reading of these works and from biases conditioned both by the kind of narrative traditionally labeled "committed" and by the tendency to approach Latin American literature from a European or North American perspective that sees the "new narrative" as a variation of the French *nouveau roman* or of the current represented in the United States by figures such as John Barth or Thomas Pynchon.

The charge that concern with form has induced Latin American writers into a kind of "play with words" which isolates the work from its context may be true of a few minor authors who, for this very reason, have never come to occupy a relevant place in the literature of the continent. Yet, when applied to the really significant writers, those that have transcended the barriers of their literature and imprinted their names among those of the great literary creators of the century (the ones we usually refer to when speaking of the authors of the "new narrative")[16] it constitutes a

---

[15] In his conversation with Vargas Llosa at the Universidad Nacional de Ingeniería in Lima, later published by Milla Batres (see n. 10), García Márquez affirms: "A los diecisiete empecé a escribirla [la narrativa de *Cien años de soledad*] y me encontré que no podía, pues me faltaban los elementos técnicos. La historia la tenía completa. Entonces necesité escribir cuatro libros para aprender a escribir *Cien años de soledad*" (p. 28).

[16] The list is long; as examples one can mention Asturias, Carpentier, Cortázar, Fuentes, G. Márquez, G. Rosa, V. Llosa, Donoso, Rulfo, Onetti, Roa Bastos, Lezama Lima.

testimony to the precariousness and immaturity of a purely "contentual" criticism that disregards language as the basis of literature. Failing to realize that the truly social element in literature is precisely the form, as George Lukács stated,[17] these critics mistake as a divorce from reality that which is specifically the search for a deeper and more authentic fusion of the word with the world, or rather of the word with all its possible correlations, and do not recognize the value of a literature that is perhaps the highest expression of this fusion in contemporary times.

The preoccupation with form on the part of the authors of the "new narrative" is not an apolitical or alienating attitude, as these critics have tended to see it, but on the contrary a conscious political undertaking which comes out of the premise that to express a revolutionary view of the world one begins by revolutionizing the means to express this view; i.e., that the revolution must start from within, from the art form itself. In a polemic with the critic Oscar Collazos, published as *Literatura en la revolución y revolución en la literatura,* Cortázar makes this point clear: "La novela revolucionaria no es solamente la que tiene un 'contenido' revolucionario, sino la que procura revolucionar la novela misma, la forma novela, y para ello utiliza todas las armas de la hipótesis de trabajo, la conjetura, la trama pluridimensional, la fractura del lenguaje."[18] But the basis for this posture had already been formulated much earlier by the Marxist critic Walter Benjamin who in his famous essay, "The Author as Producer" (1934), had declared that "the revolutionary artist should not uncritically accept the existing forces of artistic production, but should develop and revolutionize those forces, and that his task was to develop the new media that had appeared in our technological age, "as well as to tranform the older modes of artistic production."[19] As Terry Eagleton states, paraphrasing Benjamin,

> It is not just a question of pushing a revolutionary "message" through existing media; it is a question of revolutionizing the

---

[17] George Lukács, "The Evolution of Modern Drama," cit. Terry Eagleton, *Marxism and Literary Criticism* (Berkeley: Univ. of California Press, 1976), p. 20.

[18] Óscar Collazos, Julio Cortázar, and Mario Vargas Llosa, *Literatura en la revolución y revolución en la literatura: Polémica* (Mexico: Siglo XXI, 1971), p. 73.

[19] Walter Benjamin, "The Author as Producer," cit. Eagleton, p. 62.

media themselves. . . . The truly revolutionary artist . . . is never concerned with the art-object alone, but with the means of its production. "Commitment" is more than just a matter of presenting correct political opinions in one's art; it reveals itself in how far the artist reconstructs the artistic forms at his disposal, turning readers and spectators into collaborators. (Eagleton, p. 62)

It is this wider concept of commitment expressed by Benjamin which is present in Latin America's "new narrative," an art form that challenges an entire world view by questioning its own form and consequently its own character of "literariness." Most Latin American narrators of the 20's and 30's intended to question the reality they represented in their works, but they seldom succeeded in their attempt to break with the established world view because they cast their inquiries in terms of a language too closely associated with that view and, as Cortázar states, "No se puede denunciar nada si se lo hace dentro del sistema al que pertenece lo denunciado. Escribir en contra del capitalismo con el bagaje mental y el vocabulario que se derivan del capitalismo, es perder el tiempo" (*Rayuela*, p. 509). These narrators intended to be revolutionary in the sense that they criticized and denounced the status quo, but having used the language of the establishment in order to attain their aim they failed from a lack of perspective, and in the end produced one more manifestation of the system against which they were rebelling. Their art became an art of "reflection," of "mirroring," rather than one of rupture or dissention. The "new narrative," in contrast, started from the assumption that to effect an actual rupture in the system it would have to be, as Carlos Fuentes says, an art of "disorder," or rather of a possible order contrary to the dominant one, and it becomes a true revolutionary art in the sense that it "le niega al orden establecido el léxico que éste quisiera y le opone el lenguaje de la alarma, la renovación, el desorden y el humor. El lenguaje, en suma, de la ambigüedad: de la pluralidad de significados, de la constelación de alusiones: de la apertura."[20] This language is the language of searching, one of the very attributes which characterize twentieth-century man and

---

[20] Carlos Fuentes, *La nueva novela hispanoamericana* (Mexico: Cuadernos de Joaquín Mortiz, 1969), p. 32.

therefore a suitable form to express his reality. Thus, rather than alienating man from his reality, this language of rupture places him in direct relationship with it, and by causing the reader to think it transforms him from a mere spectator or consumer into a collaborator with the writer, an actual participant in the latter's creative process. Whereas the narrative of the 20's and 30's dealt with the revolution from within the establisment and did no more than offer the reader a series of static descriptions that maintained his comfortable position as a passive consumer, the "new narrative" makes this revolution real by denying a kind of art that after all was a part of the system's ideology. Hence Cortázar's claim that we need more than ever "los Che Guevara del lenguaje, los revolucionarios de la literatura más que los literatos de la revolución" (*Literatura en la revolución*, p. 76).

The revolution of language accomplished by the "new narrative" in Latin America does not imply, as these critics have inferred, the abandonment of social themes that had for so long constituted an honored trend in Latin American literature; precisely this quality distinguishes the "new narrative" from most other formalist attempts which invaded Western literature in the course of the twentieth century. The "new narrative" has always been aware of the risk of coldness and dehumanization into which these formal experiments frequently fall and, unlike them, it seldom indulges in innovative undertakings for their own sake. On the contrary, it has usually been deeply rooted in the context from which it comes and consequently it is, as the critic Andrés Amorós has said, "a la vez que innovadora, profundamente vitalista, aferrada a los problemas concretos del hombre medio: problemas sociales, y políticos, por supuesto, pues la realidad hispanoamericana no cesa de suscitarlos, pero también problemas sentimentales, vitales, de ensueño, de insatisfacción, de nostalgia, de soledad. Se consigue así, en los casos mejores, una novela que es, a la vez, obra de arte de rigurosa calidad y testimonio, implacable de una realidad social y política notoriamente defectuosa."[21]

The sociopolitical vein which was so prominent in earlier Latin American narrative continues to be an essential element in the

---

[21] Andrés Amorós, *Introducción a la novela hispanoamericana actual* (Salamanca: Anaya, 1973), pp. 22-23.

"new narrative" – the mere mention of novels like *La casa verde, Conversación en la Catedral, Cien años de soledad, Pedro Páramo, Los ríos profundos,* or *La muerte de Artemio Cruz* is sufficient evidence. The difference lies in the fact that now it is no longer the central aspect around which the entire narrative is constructed. The subordination of the aesthetic to the political in the so-called "committed" novel of Latin America has given way in the "new narrative" to an emphasis on the aesthetic, but the sociopolitical concern has not for this reason lost its impetus, nor has it been paid less attention than before. On the contrary, one can very well say with García Márquez[22] that the "new narrative" is a much more committed form of literature – in the sociological sense included – than any previous manifestation of the genre in Latin America, and this for the simple reason that the socioeconomic aspects are dealt with through the literary in such narrative and, to quote Lukács again, "we find the impress of history in the literary work precisely as *literary*, not as some superior form of social documentation" (Eagleton, p. 24). The awareness of form present in the "new narrative" has by no means weakened the sociopolitical concern of the previous generation of fictionists but rather even stressed it – for now it is present also in the narrative language itself – and has revealed that the two terms (the aesthetic and the political), rather than being in opposition, as it was traditionally supposed, complement each other and should run *pari passu* throughout the novel. This is what Carlos Fuentes means when he declares, with beautiful imagery, in the periodical *Insula*, that there are two horses, the aesthetic and the political, and that the contemporary Spanish American novelist must accomplish the difficult task of riding them both at the same time, or that perhaps these two horses are one and the same, because "toda obra literaria fiel a sus premisas y lograda en su realización, en su expresión, tiene un significado social" (Amorós, p. 23).

---

[22] Cit. J. C. Mendizábal, "*Los funerales de la Mamá Grande* de G. García Márquez. El entierro de una tradición o la resurrección de la esperanza," *Letras de Deusto*, 5 (Jan.-June 1975), 133.

4. The "Synthesis" Novel

The fusion of the aesthetic and the political of which Fuentes speaks, that is, of an aestheticist preoccupation and an active political consciousness, places the "new narrative" of Latin America in a special position in the context of Western literature, predominantly marked by an opposition between two lines of fiction that have developed an entire literary tradition – that of the "realist" novel, on the one hand, which claims art to be essentially mimesis, and that of the "aestheticist" novel on the other, conscious of its own character of fictionality, which takes art as mystery and artifice. These two trends of fiction, which have run parallel for centuries during the history of Western literature, with occasional predominance of one at the expense of the other and which have begun to merge in the works of the great innovators of the twentieth century (Proust, Joyce, Faulkner, Kafka, Thomas Mann, among others), are neutralized in Latin America's "new narrative" to give way to a literature conscious of its double condition of *sign* and *thing* at the same time or, in other words, of representation and creation, of *re-creation*. This literature magisterially combines an ethical with an aesthetic view of the world by fusing history with story and constitutes, as Rodríguez Monegal has said of it, "no sólo el más completo objeto poético para la exploración de la realidad, sino también el más rico instrumento para transmitir esa otra realidad paralela, la realidad del lenguaje" ("Una escritura revolucionaria," p. 505).

In this literature, which embraces the so-called two dimensions of literary plurisignification – temporality or the historical experience on the one hand and the deeper and more obscure strata of the human psyche on the other – the old dichotomies that for so long dominated the literary scene lose their reason for being and melt into a dialectical synthesis that can be defined as critical in the deepest sense of the word, that is, "critical" as Fuentes understands it: "elaboración antidogmática de problemas humanos" (Fuentes, p. 35). Thus imagination, rather than being in opposition to "realism," is in the "new narrative" the essential condition of a more vital realism, in the same way that aestheticism, or formal concern, constitutes the proper way to express the writer's reality, and that regionalism, or the particular, is an indispensable element to attain the universal. In the "new narrative," objective reality coexists with dream and fantasy; social or political preoccupation is coupled with structural or stylistic awareness; and local, circumstantial conflicts are fused with general, existential ones. And it is precisely this mixture of diverse elements, this fusion of apparent opposites, that constitutes the essence of this fiction, the only form capable of expressing in a deep and complete manner the relativity of our times. The "new narrative" in Latin America is at the same time regional and universal, mimetic and self-conscious, "realist" and fantastic, and it is this plural, globalizing, or, to use a better term, "synthesis" character which earns it a place of honor among the great literary creations of the twentieth century.

The "new narrative" of Latin America is a "synthesis" narrative, and as such it is ambitious, for it aspires to encompass reality in all its possible levels; it aims to be, as Fernando Aínsa has stated, "una especie de 'summa' que reúna todos los atributos."[23] And to attain its objective it makes use of every possible device, not only of the narrative genre but also of poetry, essay, drama, and other forms of writing, and offers the reader a vast kaleidoscope which, like the reality he lives in, is there to be unfolded or discovered day after day. In this type of narrative, characters and events, for example, are presented from a wide number of perspectives and in various manners, in such a way that it becomes difficult to draw conclusions about them. What the reader gets is a wide spectrum of possibilities, all with the same chances of actually happening, depending on his own perception, or rather on the way in which he relates himself to the work. And since one's perception is nothing absolute or static, but rather a fluid, ephemeral moment in constant process of transformation, what emerges from this narrative is sheer relativity. The "new narrative" in Latin America differs from previous forms of the genre on the continent, especially the *novela decimonónica* of the Realists and Naturalists, in that it is a "posing of problems," and its authors, as well as its readers, are indefatigable searchers engaged in an arduous struggle for the meaning of things. It is par excellence an art of its century – an art of synthesis and of relativity – and at the same

---

[23] Fernando Aínsa, "Algo más que un cohete-señal," *Mundo Nuevo*, March 1969, p. 73.

time a perfect representative of the continent from which it springs, a land that has been defined as a "crisol de culturas" ("melting-pot of cultures").[24]

5. THE "NEW NARRATIVE" AND THE MEDIEVAL ROMANCE OF CHIVALRY

As a mixed, amalgamated sort of art, the "new narrative" of Latin America has often been compared by critics to certain old forms of narrative such as the picaresque and the romance of chivalry, and has been referred to at times as a kind of revitalization of those forms. Indeed, if one takes a look at some of the works of this period in the continent, elements characteristic of those old genres, especially the chivalric romance, stand out immediately, and the influence exerted by this old literature is confirmed by various statements that the authors of the "new narrative" have made in interviews. The interest with which Guimarães Rosa spent long hours reading chivalric romances is known to almost every one of his critics. No secret either is the high esteem in which García Márquez holds the *Amadís de Gaula*, which he considers "uno de los grandes libros que se han escrito en la historia de la humanidad" (*La novela*, p. 17), or the importance that Vargas Llosa attributes to the fifteenth-century *Tirant lo Blanch*, a book originally written in Catalan by the Valencian Juan Martorell, which is, he declares, "la novela que a mí me gustaría escribir."[25]

From the old picaresque form Latin America's "new narrative" inherited among other things an acute sense for depicting society, and above all a tendency to violate constantly what Carpentier calls "el principio ingenuo de ser relato destinado a causar 'placer estético a los lectores,'" and consequently became "un instrumento de indagación, un modo de conocimiento de hombres y de épocas."[26] However, it is through the romances of chivalry that the

---

[24] Guillermo de Torre, "La originalidad de la literatura hispanoamericana," *Revista de Occidente*, 13 (1967), 204.
[25] Günter Lorenz, *Diálogo con América Latina* (Valparaíso: Ediciones Universitarias, 1972), p. 167.
[26] Alejo Carpentier, *Tientos y diferencias* (1967; rpt. Buenos Aires: Calicanto Editorial, 1976), p. 11.

influence of this old literature is more evidently felt, for these are, as Vargas Llosa says, "superb representations of their time," which "embrace reality on its mythical level, its religious level, its historical level, its social level, its instinctive level" (Harss and Dohmann, p. 359).

The great romances of chivalry can well be qualified with the words Vargas Llosa used in relation to his favorite, *Tirant lo Blanch*: "una novela que deslumbra tal vez antes que nada por su extraordinaria ambición, ... una tentativa de recuperación ... casi total de la realidad, ... un modelo de novela total, es decir novela que intenta describir una realidad en todos los niveles que la componen" (Lorenz, p. 167). And it is exactly this aspect which most approximates them to the "synthesis" novel of our days, though the critics who have traced parallels between the two forms continually point out similarities that go from the emphasis placed on action, drama, suspense, and quick plot development to their unlimited freedom, because of which the most everyday acts become exceptional and the most extraordinary events are converted into commonplace episodes. These aspects may all be present — and indeed most of them are — in both the chivalric romance and the "new narrative," but the great common trait which lies behind all that and justifies any comparison is their "synthesis" character, which, however different as a result of the historical circumstances under which each of these forms was produced, is undeniably present in both of them.

In this sense it is possible to affirm, as has Zunilda Gertel, that "la nueva narrativa no es un comienzo a partir de cero, sino una renovación, un retorno — el más personal, revolucionario y fecundo — de un agotado tronco novelístico secular" (*La novela hispanoamericana*, p. 10). But it is important to notice that by *retorno* is not meant a backward movement, a return to old forms of narrative that, owing to different historical circumstances, can no longer find a place in our contemporary world. The "new narrative" of Latin America has indeed looked back to its origins and has incorporated that old Iberian fictional tradition that was in hibernation during a long period of rationalist preponderance, but the synthesis it has effected is a new and wider one, which includes along with this tradition the "modern," realistic line that had its golden phase in the nineteenth century and which persisted into the first decades of the twentieth century.

6. The Phenomenon of the "Boom"

The synthesis accomplished by the "new narrative" of Latin America is, in our opinion, the major responsible element for the projection of a kind of narrative thus far confined to the boundaries of its countries into the realm of universal literature, a phenomenon that has been frequently labeled by criticism as "the boom of the Latin American novel."

This phenomenon has occupied the minds of several critics anxious to explain it who have pointed out reasons that range from merely historical, social, and economic to the aesthetic, based on the innovations the "new narrative" has introduced in the Latin American continent. Among the historical, social, and economic reasons those which seem most likely and which constitute common denominators in the opinion of a great number of critics, including the authors themselves, are: the increasingly important role of the Third World in the framing of universal consciousness, an increase of the reading public and a wider distribution of books in the continent, the professionalization of literature, the absence of a substantial group of good novelists in Europe and the United States, and the idea that the "boom" accompanies the decay of a civilization. Among the aesthetic reasons are the humanization of the landscape and universalization of the region, the expansion of the concept of reality to include levels hitherto seen as "unreal" and inferior, the aesthetic consciousness of the writer and his revitalization of language, and the emergence of a new concept of commitment, which does away with the manichaeism of the novel of protest.

Although it is undeniable that these reasons so firmly pointed out by the critics have all contributed to the so-called "boom" of the Latin American novel, it is nevertheless highly questionable whether any one of them alone may be considered sufficient to explain the phenomenon. All the historical, social, and economic reasons mentioned above do correspond to facts which have indeed played a decisive role in the expansion of this novel; however, it does not seem reasonable to believe that a literary event may be exclusively determined by causes extraneous to the works themselves. An increase in the reading public and a wider distribution of books in a continent undoubtedly contribute to the development and projection of a literature, but the result will not be significant if these factors are not accompanied by the high quality of the books. There are historical causes which create a favorable ground for the flourishing of certain literary genres – many critics have traced, for instance, a relationship between the great moments of decadence of a civilization and the appearance of significant groups of writers – but it is simplistic and naive to believe in a cause-effect relationship according to which they alone would be sufficient to explain the fact. The historical reasons are important and cannot be disregarded, but they are intimately connected with reasons of another sort, namely aesthetic, which have to do with the intrinsic aspects of the works themselves. Thus the professionalization of literature, a reason that has been mentioned by the critics as basically social or historical, constitutes a fundamental issue for its success and propagation because it allows the writers more time to elaborate their works and consequently offer their public higher-quality products. In the same way, the absence of a relevant group of writers in Europe and the United States is an important point only insofar as the novels published in Latin America are of a quality that may surpass the ones coming out in those places and therefore attract the reading public.

The aesthetic reasons pointed out by the critics as responsible for the emergence of the Latin American narrative are all fundamental aspects of this narrative that have undeniably contributed to its "boom" in the last three decades, but again none of them, if taken by itself, can be considered the unique cause. The humanization of the landscape and the consequent universalization of the region have certainly attracted the interest of readers, especially from abroad, who now – rather than placing themselves at a distance when reading a Latin American novel and seeing things and events as exotic or picturesque – can more closely accompany the characters throughout their existential itinerary, but it can not be said that this constitutes a determining factor in their choice of the books. In the same way the expansion of the concept of reality, by opening up an entirely new space which stimulates the reader's imagination and excites his thinking, has projected this novel far beyond its previous limits, but to accept this as a sole or primordial reason for the latter's success is to forget the basic assumption that realism in literature cannot be dissociated from style. The aesthetic consciousness of the writer and the revitalization of language are evidence of this fact, for here again we can say that these reasons have contributed to the "new narrative's" successful achievement only because they are intimately linked with the multiple view of the world of twentieth-century man. Thus, if one considers the linguistic and structural innovations introduced by this type of narrative as being responsible for its success, one makes the same mistake of taking one aspect as representative of the whole and fails to see that these innovations, far from being a pure entertainment, are a conscious attempt to approach reality from a different perspective, one which more closely corresponds to the contemporary world view and to a concept of commitment which sees man as a dynamic force in relation to a world in a constant process of mutation.

But if none of these reasons alone can be considered responsible for projecting the Latin American novel into world literature, the synthesis the "new narrative" has effected by fusing these various aspects constitutes a strong argument for our view of the issue. The critic Rodríguez Monegal seems to have recognized this in an article in which, after praising the linguistic and structural innovations brought about by this narrative, he states that the latter's success does not depend exclusively on that but also on the fact that it alludes to extraliterary realities, in a clear reference to the historical environment represented in the genre.[27] Although this is just one aspect of the "synthesis" effected by the "new narrative" – the fusion of a high aesthetic consciousness with the elements of the outer world which it is intended to represent – the affirmation made by the critic gives credit to the assumption that the novel must embrace reality in as many of its facets as possible, and that its success or failure is contingent above all upon the way in which it has realized this purpose. And since the "new narrative" has undoubtedly attained a high level in this sense, recognition of which has led several critics to assert that Latin American narrative has finally reached its maturity, it is not irrelevant to insist here that it is above all the novel's "synthesis" character that explains the phenomenon of its "boom."

---

[27] Emir Rodríguez Monegal, "Latin American Literature," in *World Literature since 1945*, ed. Ivan Ivask and Gero von Wilpert (New York: Frederick Ungar, 1973), p. 441.

7. Revitalization of the Novel Genre

Another important aspect of the "synthesis" effected by the "new narrative" of Latin America is that it constitutes a challenge to the argument that the novel is dead. This argument, first used in relation to the Modernist European writers of the early twentieth century, was later generalized by critics who, though varying sometimes in their position as to whether a certain book, such as *Ulysses* or *To the Lighthouse*, could or could not be considered a novel, were in agreement when accusing the contemporary manifestations of the genre of "unrealism," because of what they called their excessive formalism and subjectivism. Those critics who supported and defended the argument, though coming from different schools and varied literary backgrounds, all shared the vision that the novel was associated with the bourgeoisie and its literary counterpart – objective realism – and consequently was "too rooted in a vanishing phase of history and society to be able to grasp contemporary reality."[28]

Although this issue is too long and controversial to discuss in detail here, it is necessary to state that these critics, apart from their different argumentation, all committed the same serious mistake of approaching the subject with a monocular vision which failed to see the dialectics existing between art and reality and restricted the scope of the novel by denying its capacity for revitalizing itself. The relationship between art and reality contains that which Bernard Pinguaud has called "the law of growing realism," which consists of a permanent effort to capture and transmit a reality which is changeable and, therefore, can be expressed only through forms that also evolve (cit. Aínsa, p. 71). As nothing is fixed in the world, it is impossible to conceive of a form of literature which maintains a firm and inflexible relationship with reality. There is no doubt that the novel as a literary genre has gone through an important crisis in the course of the twentieth century, a crisis that has come as a consequence of the immense transformation the world has experienced in this period,

---

[28] Bernard Bergonzi, *The Situation of the Novel*, Critical Essays in Modern Literature, 2d ed. (Pittsburgh: Univ. of Pittsburgh Press, 1972), p. 14, paraphrasing George Steiner.

but to affirm, as those critics have, that the novel is no longer alive is to deny the evolutionary character of art and reduce it to fixed labels. What is dead, we may say with Carlos Fuentes, "no es la novela, sino precisamente la forma burguesa de la novela y su término de referencia, el realismo, que supone un estilo descriptivo y sicológico de observar a individuos en relaciones personales y sociales" (Fuentes, p. 17). But if "bourgeois realism" is dead, this by no means implies that novelistic reality has perished with it. On the contrary, and again it is Fuentes who states:

> Inmersos en esta crisis, pero indicando ya el camino para salir de ella, varios grandes novelistas han demostrado que la muerte del realismo burgués sólo anuncia el advenimiento de una realidad literaria mucho más poderosa... [que] se expresa... en la capacidad para encontrar y levantar sobre un lenguaje los mitos y las profecías de una época cuyo verdadero sello no es la dicotomía capitalismo-socialismo, sino una suma de hechos... que realmente están transformando la vida en las sociedades industriales: automatización, electrónica, uso pacífico de energía atómica. (Fuentes, pp. 17-18)

The novel form in the twentieth century, rather than having died, is a reality which has survived thanks precisely to the genre's capacity for redefining itself, an aspect which is part of its own essence – novelty – and the transformations it has gone through, far from being a sign of its moribundity, are an expression of the changes taking place in Western thought. As the concept of reality has evolved from an absolutist to a relativistic perspective, so the novel has abandoned its condition of being merely "a verisimilar representation of moral situations in their social context,"[29] and has become an object of search, of investigation, which includes other possible levels of reality. Conscious that objective reality is simply one aspect of reality, not the whole of it, as the scientific mentality of the second half of the nineteenth century believed, the contemporary novel has transcended "objective realism" and projected itself into a new dimension, characterized precisely by a will to represent reality in as many of its aspects as possible.

---

[29] Robert Alter, *Partial Magic: The Novel as a Self-Conscious Genre* (Berkeley: Univ. of California Press, 1975), p. ix.

But this will for totality, so relevant for the twentieth-century novel, is not always present in all its manifestations, and for this very reason it constitutes an aspect which distinguishes the "new narrative" of Latin America from certain contemporary forms of the genre in Europe and the United States. The critics who condemn the contemporary novel for its excessive formalism or subjectivism are usually addressing their words to some of these latter forms, but their error lies in the fact that their argument implies a generalization that indicates either an ignorance of other literatures or a prejudiced, narrow-minded conception that considers the categories of their cultures to be universal. For if this sort of blame can be laid to those novel forms, it can by no means apply to the "new narrative" of Latin America, in which those aspects not only are in equilibrium but also are not used for their own sake. Subjectivism, which has driven the Surrealist European writers into incommunicable islands, far from being a dominant trait in this narrative, is simply one aspect of the reality represented. And the formal preoccupation, responsible for the dehumanization (to use Ortega y Gasset's term) of so many well-intentioned literary attempts such as the French *nouveau roman*, is in the "new narrative" of Latin America a successful effort at revitalization, accomplished with the clear purpose of making the genre capable of grasping as completely as possible the reality of twentieth-century man. The "new narrative" of Latin America, unlike those other forms condemned by these critics, has always made use of the elements of subjectivism and formalism with the intent to represent reality in its widest sense, and by such means it has accomplished a revitalization of the genre which proves its continuity. Thus we can say, with the Brazilian critic Leandro Konder in his introduction to the Portuguese translation of Ferenc Fehér's study *O romance está morrendo?*, that "apesar do *Ulysses*, apesar do empenho das sucessivas ondas 'vanguardistas,' apesar de Adorno e Goldmann, apesar do 'antiromance' e apesar das debilidades dos defensores dos romances, o gênero sobreviveu,"[30] and unhesitatingly cite, as he has, the Latin American novel as a reliable example.

---

[30] Leandro Konder, "Uma nova teoria do romance," in *O romance está morrendo?* by Ferenc Fehér, trans. Eduardo Lima (Rio de Janeiro: Paz e Terra, 1972), p. xix.

The "new narrative" of Latin America, though it has suffered a certain amount of influence from the various European and North American currents of the twentieth century, differs from them precisely because of its "synthesis" character, which makes of it a literature conscious of its own condition of fictionality, a literature that emphasizes this quality to the utmost limit, but at the same time a form which in any case never loses contact with its function of representing reality. This "new narrative" is a literary form deeply rooted in the reality from where it springs, a reality which is, on its turn, as Fernando Alegría once affirmed, in a constant state of revolution. Thus, more than being a pure expression of discontent, which either reflects in a static way the apparent side of things or throws man into a kind of no exit labyrinth, it constitutes an integral part of this revolution – accomplished within its own form – and calls for a kind of participation comparable only to that urged, in the great moments of the genre, by figures who imprinted their names in the history of Western literature.

This "synthesis" narrative which has effected a revolution of the genre that reflects and at the same time represents the revolution of society in its ongoing process and fulfilled well its task of revelation, by questioning and inducing the reader to put to question every single aspect of reality, will be the object of study in the following section. For this purpose we will focus on a novel which, not only is highly significant in this sense, but also constitutes an exponent of both Brazilian and Latin American literature as a whole – namely, Guimarães Rosa's *Grande sertão: veredas*.

PART II

JOÃO GUIMARÃES ROSA'S *GRANDE SERTÃO: VEREDAS*

> Todos os meus livros são simples tentativas de rodear e devassar um pouquinho o mistério cósmico, esta coisa movente, rebelde a qualquer lógica, que é a chamada "realidade," que é a gente mesmo, o mundo, a vida. Antes o obscuro que o óbvio, que o frouxo. Toda lógica contém inevitável dose de mistificação. Toda mistificação contém boa dose de verdade. Precisamos também do obscuro.
>
> JOÃO GUIMARÃES ROSA

1. *GRANDE SERTÃO: VEREDAS*: A "SYNTHESIS" NOVEL

João Guimarães Rosa's first and only novel — *Grande sertão: veredas* — was published in Brazil in 1956. Since then it has received a large number of reviews and a considerable amount of critical studies that range from mere praise or detraction to substantial works which focus on the novel with reasonable depth and offer the reader useful assistance in penetrating the author's fictitious universe. These more serious studies, which undoubtedly constitute a great contribution to the understanding and appreciation of the novel, are usually of two kinds — a large number of linguistic or philological analyses which aim at explaining the text, and a smaller number of works which — though also concerned with these linguistic aspects — transcend the purely exegetic level and attempt to offer some interpretation of the novel's thematic structure.[1]

---

[1] A wide selection of these studies can be found in *Guimarães Rosa*, ed. Eduardo de Faria Coutinho, Fortuna Crítica, 6 (Rio de Janeiro: Civilização Brasileira, 1983).

Although these two kinds of criticism differ substantially in their approach and aims – the former is concerned merely with breaking the language barrier created between the reader and the text as a result of the author's use of a type of language never before employed in any Brazilian novel, and the latter with describing and interpreting the novel as a whole – a common denominator can be pointed out in all these studies, which is the recognition that both the very language of the novel and its structure as a whole are a synthesis of various elements, frequently opposed to each other, that coexist and interpenetrate to form that totality which is the body of *Grande sertão: veredas*. This is why it is perfectly accurate to state, as Harss has done in the chapter dedicated to Rosa in *Into the Mainstream*, that the novel is "not just a world, but a whole cosmos. It is a terminal book, a Summa. It touches on all the points of the compass to become a total experience that engages the reader at every level. It did the author, too. He put everything he had into it" (p. 164).

The majority of the linguistic and philological studies of *Grande sertão: veredas*, varied as they may be, are all in perfect agreement that the language used in the novel, far from being a faithful reproduction of any specific dialect spoken in Brazil, is an aesthetic creation composed of the amalgamation of the various dialects existing in the country plus a series of contributions either coming from foreign languages, including classical Greek and Latin, or resulting from the author's own capacity for inventing or recreating entire new words and expressions. The vocabulary of the novel, to take just one example on this linguistic level, is a hybrid creation, formed by the harmonious coexistence of terms apparently incompatible, such as regionalisms and foreign words, archaisms and neologisms, erudite and colloquial terms or expressions. These elements not only are all present in *Grande sertão: veredas* but are sometimes fused into a new word which comes about as the product of this mixture and serves perhaps better than any other aspect of the language of the novel to illustrate the aesthetic achievements of Guimarães Rosa. They are portmanteau words, a type so dear to Lewis Carroll and later abundantly used by Joyce in *Ulysses* and *Finnegans Wake*.

In the same way, the other kind of substantial studies written about *Grande sertão: veredas*, the texts which offer a description of the narrative mechanism of the work and attempt to interpret its thematic structure, all reveal the common belief that ambiguity constitutes the basic structural principle in the novel. It is the basis of the narrative's thematic structure, which is composed of a series of opposing pairs (good: evil, essence: appearance, to be: not to be) whose terms coexist in constant tension and are fused at the end into a dialectical synthesis, indicated by the leitmotif *Tudo é e não é* ("Everything is and is not") repeated a great number of times in the book. Besides, it is an element present at every level of the narrative, including the formal structure of the tale, whose movement constantly oscillates between two opposing but not exclusive terms. These terms – *viver* and *contar* ("living" and "narrating"), represented by the leitmotifs *Viver é muito perigoso* and *Contar é muito, muito dificultoso* ("Living is very dangerous" and "Narrating is very, very difficult") – also merge at the end into a synthesis that suggests an identification between the process of living and that of narrating a novel.

But this synthesis, present at every level of the narrative of *Grande sertão: veredas*, including language itself, and responsible for making of it a "total" novel in the sense mentioned by Harss, does not embrace all the aspects of the synthesis with which we are concerned here. *Grande sertão: veredas* is a synthesis novel also because it fuses in its corpus a series of antinomic elements which represent different traditional trends of both Brazilian and Latin American literature as a whole, such as regionalism and universalism, objectivism and subjectivism, aestheticism and social commitment. These elements, which were formerly seen as antagonistic and even served as points of reference for superficial classifications based on the predominance of one of them at the expense of the other, are now employed in perfect balance in *Grande sertão: veredas*, and the opposition previously existing between them is neutralized. In this section we will study the presence of each of these elements at the different levels of the narrative of *Grande sertão: veredas* and will see how their previous antagonism is replaced by a perfect harmony, according to which, rather than being in opposition, they complement each other in the whole of the novel. This fusion of the traditionally opposing tendencies of Latin American literature constitutes, in our view, one of the greatest contributions of Rosa's novel to the literary panorama of the continent.

2. CHARACTER AND SPACE IN *GRANDE SERTÃO: VEREDAS*

> En el Sertão se habla el idioma de Goethe, Dostoyevski y Flaubert, visto no desde lo filológico sino desde lo metafísico, porque el Sertão es el terreno de la eternidad, de la soledad, donde *Inneres und Äusseres sind nicht mehr zu trennen* [lo interior y lo exterior ya son inseparables], según el *Westöstlicher Diván* [el diván oriental-occidental].
>
> JOÃO GUIMARÃES ROSA

2.1. *The Jagunço Riobaldo*

We have seen in the first section of this study that one of the aspects which best characterizes the "new narrative" of Latin America is its condition of being at the same time regional and universal as a result of a shift in the novel's center of gravity from nature to man or, in other words, from a purely regionalist to a more nearly universal perspective, according to which the regional elements, though still highly significant, no longer form by themselves the core of the work. This shift — which consists above all in a humanization of the landscape in the sense that man rather than the landscape now is the pivotal element and reflects a new maturity on the part of the novelist, who no longer sees his land as a special, isolated case but as a part of a wider complex that can be named the Western world — has introduced important innovations into the text of the novel, among which the emergence of a new kind of hero, who replaces the pure "type" of the regionalist novel, and the universalization of the region. Since these two aspects are of primary importance in the framework of *Grande sertão: veredas* and have to do with two fundamental elements of any type of fiction — character and space — we will center around them our discussion on the neutralization of the opposition between regionalism and universalism in this novel, and will mention the other aspects of the narrative insofar as they are directly or indirectly related to them.

Reading *Grande sertão: veredas* for the first time, one is immediately struck by the ambiguity of the narrator-protagonist of the novel, who is, and at the same time is not, a jagunço.[2] The narrative of *Grande sertão: veredas* is the report of his former life as a jagunço made by Riobaldo, now an old farmer, to a cultivated urban citizen traveling through the Brazilian backlands. Yet throughout the entire narrative the reader clearly feels that the protagonist, though having led for a long time the life of a jagunço, has never completely identified with the model, at least as it is presented by the other jagunços in the novel: "Eu era muito diverso deles todos, que sim. Então eu não era jagunço completo, estava ali no meio executando um erro," he says to his interlocutor, and adds: "Tudo receei. Eles não pensavam" (338).

This consciousness that he was different from his companions, that he was "mesmo de outras extrações" (157), has always given Riobaldo a feeling that he was an outsider among them, that he did not belong in that world, as is evidenced in the following passage, in which he comments on the attitude of a group of jagunços towards him: "Ao às tantas me aceitaram; mas meio atalhados. Se o que fossem mesmo de constância assim, por tempero de propensão; ou, então, por me arrediarem, porquanto me achando deles diverso?" (156). Riobaldo is aware that he is not like the other jagunços and he clearly affirms that – "A verdade que diga, eu achava que não tinha nascido para aquilo, de ser sempre jagunço não gostava" (65) – yet he enters the jagunços' world and shares their life experience to such an extent that he finally becomes not only his group's leader but also the only man capable of restoring to that group the equilibrium upset by the treacherous murder of its first charismatic leader, Joca Ramiro.

But during his entire life as a jagunço, Riobaldo has never completely adapted to his companions' way of life, and has always maintained a distance in relation to them: "Por simples que a companheirada naqueles tempos me caceteava com um enjôo, todos eu achava muito ignorantes, grosseiros cabras" (61), he says, and at another moment remarks: "Acho que sempre desgostei de criaturas que com pouco e fácil se contentam" (142). The typical jagunços were pure men of action, men who merely obeyed the orders of a leader and never even wondered about the reasons for their acts. They were men who practically did not think, as is

---

[2] The term *jagunço* is applied in Brazilian Portuguese to a member of a group of outlaws, inhabitants of the backlands, who form a sort of bodyguard to defend either their own interests or those of the landowners that support them.

made clear in the following passages in which Riobaldo states: "E os outros, companheiros, que é que os outros pensavam? Sei? De certo nadas e noves – iam como o costume – sertanejos tão sofridos. Jagunço é homem já meio desistido por si" (50) and "Não podendo entender a razão da vida, é só assim que se pode ser vero bom jagunço" (537).

Riobaldo, in contrast with his companions, is a man of thought, a speculative being, and it is this very quality which confers individuality upon him and accounts for his transcendence of the jagunço type. Whereas the other jagunços simply accept their status as puppets manipulated by wealthy and powerful landowners who offter them support in exchange for their services, he is always questioning his condition as a jagunço and constantly seeking a meaning to his actions. Thus while searching for Zé Bebelo and the government's soldiers, under the leadership of Hermógenes, he asks himself why he is obliged to obey that man: "Eu tinha de obedecer a ele, fazer o que mandasse. Mandava matar. Meu querer não correspondia ali, por conta nenhuma. Eu nem conhecia aqueles inimigos, tinha raiva nenhuma deles.... Por que era que eu tinha de obedecer ao Hermógenes?" (197-98); and, a little later, during the combat, he questions the very necessity of the fight, remarking: "Andando que aquele ataque nosso não servia para resultado nenhum, e eu carecia de avistar os outros, saber de qualquer contagem de balanço, de quantos tinham morrido ou estavam mal. Eu queria saber dos deles e dos nossos. Combate sem cabimento! Só o tiroteio, repetido reproduzido" (203).

The passages above clearly express the gap existing between Riobaldo and the jagunço's world, for by questioning the necessity to obey the orders of his superior and the validity of the latter's decisions he is contravening the very code that rules that world. This code requires unquestioned obedience and complete submission to the will and decisions of a leader, yet Riobaldo refuses to accept these values as a natural imposition. It is true he fulfills his duty as a jagunço by participating in the combat as much as his companions, but by his questioning he transcends the pure type and places himself in a position far beyond the limitations imposed by that world. That is why he asks himself later in his life: "O jagunço Riobaldo. Fui eu?" and replies: "Fui e não fui. Não fui. Não fui! – porque não sou, não quero ser. Deus esteja" (206). If to be a jagunço means to attain completely a specific ethical code and to restrict one's activities to a typical way of life, without questioning any of the reasons and validity of one's acts, then Riobaldo is right when affirming so insistently that he has not been one. But is that all it means to be a jagunço?

It is important to note here that Riobaldo's speculative character by no means excludes his status as a man of action. The protagonist of *Grande sertão: veredas* is, as the critic José Carlos Garbuglio has said in his study *O mundo movente de Guimarães Rosa*, at the same time a man of action and a man of thought,[3] and it is precisely of this duplexity that the essence of the character consists. It is true that by his questioning Riobaldo transcends the type and becomes a complex character, endowed with a wide human dimension, but in so doing he does not entirely lose track of his condition as a type, for his speculations cannot be dissociated from his life as a jagunço. On the contrary, they are a consequence of that life, or in other words they come as a result of the gap existing between himself as an individual and the life he leads.

This gap, reponsible for throwing Riobaldo first into a desperate search for the meaning of his acts and later into a whole speculative process aimed at self-justification, appears very early in his life under the contradictory form of an attraction to and at the same time a repulsion against the jagunço's way of life. Since his adolescence, when he had his first contact with a group of jagunços that had spent a day at his godfather's farm, he felt enormously attracted to their way of life and nourished the hope of joining them one day. Yet a moral consciousness, deriving from his earlier life with his mother and his experience in the little town where he had been sent to receive some education, among other things always worked as an opposing force and prevented his dream from coming true. Riobaldo already at that time believed, as he later confesses that "quem de si de ser jagunço se entrete, já é por alguma competência entrante do demônio" (11), and with that in mind he lets his life take a different direction. But chance plays a trick on him and he eventually runs into exactly that from which he was trying to escape: he accepts a job as a private instructor to

---

[3] José Carlos Garbuglio, *O mundo movente de Guimarães Rosa* (São Paulo: Ática, 1972).

a man who happened to be fighting the jagunços, and through him is introduced to their nomadic life.

At this point, the character's inner conflict is intensified: Riobaldo admires the jagunços, but takes part in a group whose aim is to exterminate them; he does not want to lead the life of a jagunço, yet his life in the adversary group does not differ much from it. Conscious of these contradictions, he deserts his group, only to fall once more into the hands of destiny: he comes across a young man who years before had exerted a strange fascination over him and who now, as a jagunço, leads him to join his group. At this moment Riobaldo's life as a jagunço starts. Now he belongs to a group, receives orders from a leader, and will kill or die according to fixed precepts. Yet he is not happy with that and frequently asks himself:

> Que é que eu era? Um raso jagunço atirador, cachorrando por este sertão. O mais que eu podia ter sido capaz de pelejar certo, de ser e de fazer; e no real eu não conseguia. Só a continuação de airagem, trastejo, trançar o vazio. Mas, por que? – eu pensava. Ah, então, sempre achei: por causa de minha costumação, e por causa dos outros. Os outros, os companheiros, que viviam à toa, desestribados; e viviam perto da gente demais, desgovernavam toda-a-hora a atenção, a certeza de se ser, a segurança destemida, e o alto destino possível da gente. De que é que adiantava, se não, estatuto de jagunço? Ah, era. Por isso, eu tinha grande desprezo de mim, e tinha cisma de todo o mundo. (381)

But Riobaldo's career as a jagunço does not stop there and the conflict, represented by the opposition between accepting that way of life and looking for another one, develops into a new phase which requires greater responsability. Now the question posed to him is whether to become the leader of his group. Riobaldo's ability as a great shooter is immediately noticed by his companions and his capacity for being their leader is recognized even by the leaders themselves, who so indicate at two important moments. First it is Joca Ramiro, whose murder provokes the scission of the jagunços' group and calls for revenge, who exclaims when being introduced to him: "Meu filho, você tem as marcas de conciso valente" (236) and gives him a rifle, a symbolic present. Second is Medeiro Vaz, Ramiro's immediate successor, notorious for his bravery and strategies for fighting, who from his deathbed extends his finger to him, expressing the desire that he be the man to take his place. Yet Riobaldo does not want to accept that position, and tries as much as he can to escape from it. But as the war develops among the jagunços and the moments of risk become more frequent and tougher, that which seemed to him merely incidental is revealed as a heavy moral duty. By this time, Riobaldo is already committed to the jagunços' cause, and feels that he must do whatever is necessary to defend it. The jagunços are marching, under the command of Zé Bebelo, to combat Hermógenes, the traitor, but their leader, though very capable and apparently well intentioned, has committed a series of mistakes. Thus Riobaldo, realizing that under the circumstances he is the only one capable of achieving the goal for which they are striving, decides to take over the command of the troops.

His decision, however, does not come easily. A Hamlet-like character, Riobaldo is divided between his dedication to the jagunços' cause and his own moral principles, according to which the position of jagunço chief implies a great amount of evil, and while conscious that he can no longer turn back he feels weak and hesitates. To find strength to take on that which he now sees as his doom, Riobaldo makes a pact with the devil one midnight at a certain crossroad. But this episode, a turning point in the character's existential itinerary, rather than eliminating his conflict replaces it with another, now of a different kind. Having confronted the forces of evil, Riobaldo feels capable of assuming the leadership of his group, and as a leader commits himself so fully to his role that he brings the war to a decisive battle which ends in the group's victory. Yet, though victorious, he is far from feeling satisfied or fulfilled; a strong feeling of guilt, resulting from the belief that he had sold his soul to the devil, will torment him for rest of his life.

This guilty feeling constitutes the basis for Riobaldo's later metaphysical speculations, which in turn motivate his narration of his life to his interlocutor. This motivation is made very explicit when, for example, he says: "Não tenciono relatar ao senhor minha vida em dobrados passos; servia para quê? Quero é armar o ponto dum fato, para depois lhe pedir um conselho. Por daí, então, careço de que o senhor escute bem essas passagens: da vida de Riobaldo, o jagunço" (205-06). The "ponto dum fato" to which he refers, though not specified in the passage, is formulated throughout the entire narrative in the question repeated a great number of times about the existence of the devil. Riobaldo is tormented by the idea that he has sold his soul to the devil and wants to find out whether the latter actually exists or is, as he wants to believe, a "falso imaginado." He begins his narrative by reporting the episode of a strange appearance which people believe was the devil and finishes it with a conclusion that, if not totally convincing from the point of view of the character's process of self-justification, at least provides his conscience with some kind of relief: "Amável o senhor me ouviu, minha idéia confirmou: que o Diabo não existe. Pois não ... Nonada. O diabo não há! É o que eu digo, se for... Existe é homem humano Travessia" (571).

In spite of the phrases "pois não" ("isn't that so?") and "se for," ("if it really is") which leave the matter open for further speculation, Riobaldo denies in this passage the existence of the devil as an external entity. And by affirming that what exists is "homem humano" he implies that evil, as well as good, is a part of human essence, which is characterized precisely by the coexistence of opposing poles. This conclusion, obvious as it may seem, constitutes a decisive step in the character's process of attaining self-knowledge and reveals an acceptance of his own human condition. In his speculation Riobaldo has evolved from a Manicheist perspective, expressed by statements such as "Eu careço de que o bom seja bom e o ruim ruim, que dum lado esteja o preto e do outro o branco, que o feio fique bem apartado do bonito e a alegria longe da tristeza" (210), to a more mature view based on the relativity and reversibility of things, and at this stage his actions as a jagunço come to be seen from a different angle, stripped of their purely mythical, diabolical character. Now the man of thought, having meditated upon his former deeds, accepts the man of action, and the distinction which until then had prevailed between them disappears.

The symbol of this fusion between Riobaldo the man and Riobaldo the jagunço is present throughout the entire novel in a series of embedded stories centered around the theme of the reversibility of good and evil — the stories of Pedro Pindó, of Aleixo, and especially of Maria Mutema — but it can perhaps be best exemplified in the following extract, in which the narrator makes a reference to two kinds of manioc that, although apparently antinomic, are very similar in their essence: "Melhor, se arrepare: pois, num chão, e com igual formato de ramos e folhas, não dá a mandioca mansa, que se come comum, e a mandioca-brava, que mata? Agora, o senhor já viu uma estranhez? A mandioca-doce pode de repente virar azangada... vai em amargando, de tanto em tanto, de si mesma toma peçonhas. E, ora veja: a outra, a mandioca-brava, também é que às vezes pode ficar mansa, a esmo de se comer sem nenhum mal" (12). In the same way that the sweet, edible manioc can be poisonous sometimes and the poisonous kind can become good for eating, the man who considers the actions of a jagunço to be evil can also commit such actions without being essentially bad, and thus be at the same time a jagunço and one who questions the validity of the jagunço lifestyle.

At this point we come to an important aspect which requires further discussion: the jagunço portrayed by the narrator in *Grande sertão: veredas* is by no means a type constructed exclusively along a negative semantic axis. It is true that the jagunços frequently appear in the novel as bandits involved in a series of evil actions, as for example when Riobaldo describes their life at Hermógenes' campground, or when he reports their cruelties when invading small villages: "... baleando, esfaqueando, estripando, furando os olhos, cortando línguas e orelhas, não economizando as crianças pequenas, atirando na inocência do gado, queimado pessoas ainda meio vivas, na beira de estrago de sangues" (48). But at the same time they are presented as soldiers, and even heroes, victims of a complex social situation, capable of a number of noble actions, who kill and die out of loyalty to their leader and above all to an ethical code which, though different from the dominant one, is not shown as hierarchally inferior. In the name of this code, which aims at a noble cause – to bring justice, insofar as possible, to the backlands – the jagunço commits many atrocities, but by manipulating evil as a condition to attain good he transcends, as the critic Antônio Cândido affirms, the status of a pure bandit.[4] Far from being a common criminal, the jagunço is represented as a multiple, contradictory being, also endowed with a heroic status wich places

---

[4] Antônio Cândido, "Jagunços mineiros de Cláudio a Guimarães Rosa," in *Vários escritos* (São Paulo: Livraria Duas Cidades, 1970), pp. 133-60.

him in a position very similar to that of the heroes of the medieval romances of chivalry.

This positive, heroic side of the jagunço is evidenced in *Grande sertão: veredas* by a series of references made to his courage, loyalty, and perseverance, as in the following passage, which comes after a disastrous attempt at crossing the Liso do Sussuarão, a gorge that no other troop had yet succeeded in crossing: "Esbandalhados nós estávamos, escatimados naquela esfrega. Esmorecidos é que não. Nenhum se lastimava, filhos do dia, acho mesmo que ninguém se dizia de dar por assim. Jagunço é isso. Jagunço não se escabreia com perda nem derrota – quase que tudo para ele é o igual" (55); or in another extract which contains a clear allusion to the jagunço's pride and potential for sensitivity:

> Assim apreciei a gente – às mansas e às bravas – a minha jagunçada. Agora eles estavam arrumando o mundo de outra maneira. Tudo se media munição, e era fuzil e rifle se experimentando. A guerra era de todos. A juízo, eu não devia de mestrear demais, tudo prescrevendo: porque eles também tinham melindre para se desgostar ou ofender, como jagunço sabe honra de profissão. Dos modos deles, próprios, era que eu podia me saber, certificado, ver a preço, se eu estava para ser e sendo exato chefe. (539)

But at no other moment are the jagunço's bravery and sense of honor made more explicit than when Riobaldo, realizing that S. Habão, a farmer on whose lands the group is temporarily camping, intended to hire the jagunços as workers, comments: "Até enjoei. Os jagunços destemidos, arriscando a vida, que nós éramos; e aquele S. Habão olhava feito o jacaré no juncal: cobiçava a gente para escravos!" (392).

This impetuosity of the jagunço, who lives in constant risk, his desire for glory and reputation, and his loyalty toward his leader and his companions, among other qualities, endow him with a strong dose of idealism which makes of him rather a modern version of the knights of the romances of chivalry. However, his lack of perspective on life, constantly pointed out by Riobaldo, and his servility and submission to the figure of the wealthy landowners, reveal him as a social outcast whose survival depends entirely on the will of these men. The jagunços present in *Grande sertão: veredas*, ideal as they may be, are also a faithful reproduction of the class existing in the Brazilian backlands, which Walnice Nogueira Galvão, in *As formas do falso*, designates as the "retainers" – that is, a huge group of people who, having no other means of subsistence, live under the protection of powerful proprietors who in exchange use their services, ranging from votes in elections to combat against any force that might threaten their stability.[5]

The dependence of the jagunços on the powerful landowners is referred to several times by the narrator in *Grande sertão: veredas* through comments such as:

> Ah, a vida vera é outra, do cidadão do sertão. Política! Tudo política, e potentes chefias. A pena, que aqui já é terra avinda concorde, roncice de paz, e sou homem particular. Mas, adiante, por aí arriba, ainda fazendeiro graúdo se reina mandador – todos donos de agregados valentes, turmas de cabras no trabuco e na carabina escopetada! Domingos Touro, no Alambiques, Major Urbano no Macaçá, os Silva Salles na Crondeúba, no Vau-Vau dona Próspera Blaziana.... e tantos, tantos. Nisto que na extrema de cada fazenda some e surge um camarada, de sentinela, que sobraça o pau-de-fogo e vigia feito onça que come carcaça. (107)

It is made even more explicit when Riobaldo mentions that his leaders all receive money and supplies from powerful politicians, proprietors of extensive pieces of land, who associate with them for the purpose of maintaining their power and a status quo extremely favorable to them. As a matter of fact, most of the leaders themselves are wealthy landowners who on the one hand experience the life of the jagunços by participating in their marches and sharing their ideal of glory and fame, and on the other hand are like the great proprietors, defending their own interests and striving to maintain a situation in which the only victim is the jagunço himself. To be sure, there are exceptions among them, such as Medeiro Vaz, perhaps the most idealistic figure in the novel, who gives up his properties and position to devote himself entirely to the jagunços' cause. But it is important to note that a difference is clearly made in *Grande sertão: veredas* between the leaders of the

---

[5] Walnice Nogueira Galvão, *As formas do falso* (São Paulo: Perspectiva, 1972).

groups, who have their own means of subsistence and are sometimes prestigious among their men for this very reason, and the jagunços themselves. The latter are mere soldiers, unconscious of their own position and contradictions, "homens provisórios," in the words of Riobaldo, who risk their life at every moment to support a state of things, based on individual economic power and prestige, which does not bring them any true profit or advantage. They are, as Nogueira Galvão has said, the "utilized useless" – useless as a consequence of their alienation from the basic means of production in the society in which they live and utilized or exploited for this very reason by the same society which marginalizes them.

A contradictory being, bandit and at the same time hero, capable of extreme actions that range from vile to noble, soldier and social outcast, defender of a society which exploits him for his valor and condemns him for his actions – this is the jagunço one finds in the pages of *Grande sertão: veredas:* a social type based on a concrete reality, the jagunço so common in the Brazilian backlands, and an ideal, fictitious creation, molded in great part on the heroes of the romances of chivalry, whose values still live in the popular and folkloric tradition of the inhabitants of these lands. This ambiguity of the jagunço type, which makes Riobaldo constantly oscillate in his desire for and at the same time repulsion against identifying with it and generates his entire process of questioning the jagunço condition itself, is what distinguishes the type represented in *Grande sertão: veredas* from that encountered in earlier Brazilian literary works. Whereas in the latter the jagunço was portrayed from a one-sided perspective and appeared as either a hero or a social victim, in Rosa's novel he is a multiple, contradictory being who can be defined as the synthesis of the previously opposing views.

The ambiguity present in the figure of the narrator-protagonist, who embodies the type but at the same time transcends it by means of a questioning that reflects an existential conflict characteristic of twentieth-century man, is also present in the type itself which, though obviously constructed around a series of clichés, transcends the one-sided perspective of the previous regionalist fiction and is projected on a larger scale, thus becoming a sign of the regional within the universal.

2.2. The Sertão and the World

In the same way that the protagonist of *Grande sertão: veredas* is simultaneously a regional type and a universal character who transcends his typicality by means of the human dimension with which he is endowed, the sertão,[6] we encounter in the pages of Rosa's novel is a multiple, ambiguous region which corresponds on one level to a physical, geographical area located in the Brazilian backlands and on another to an inner, spiritual or psychological reality with no external boundaries which can be seen as a microcosm of the world. It is true that Guimarães Rosa started the process of representing reality from a concrete region where he had spent a great part of his life and transformed or re-created this region to form the universe of his novel. But it is important to note that, in so doing, he never lost track completely of that reality which served as the point of departure. On the contrary, such a reality is present in all its rawness and concreteness, and that is what constitutes the documental side of his work, so insistently pointed out and much appreciated by sociologists of literature.

As a concrete region, the sertão here is a representation, as nearly as possible, of a specific area of the Brazilian backlands including northwestern Minas Gerais, southwestern Bahia, and southeastern Goiás. This precision is so clearly indicated in the novel by references to cities, towns, and geographical characteristics that have the same name as actual places and features that it has been possible, as the critic Alan Viggiano has done in *Itinerário de Riobaldo Tatarana*,[7] to trace the route of the narrator's marches as a jagunço in those lands. The area is depicted in all its possible aspects, from merely physical or geographical, such as its fauna, flora, climate, and hydrography, to the customs of its people and the social and economic system in which they live, and everything has been done so accurately and with such a sense of verisimilitude that anyone familiar with the region will easily recognize it. One

---

[6] *Sertão* is a geographical denomination which refers to a vast area of the Brazilian backlands. Guimarães Rosa's use of the term, which appears in the very title of the novel, will be widely discussed in the present section of this study.

[7] Alan Viggiano, *Itinerário de Riobaldo Tatarana* (Rio de Janeiro: José Olympio, 1978).

who wishes to study the novel from the point of view of a documentary will find a wide range of useful material: long lists of animals and plants abundant in the area; references about the river system and the distribution of rain in the region; the cultural habits and idiosyncrasies of the people – their typical food, mysticism, way of relating to others, beliefs and entertainments, social principles and class structure, and their basic means of survival.

For our purposes it is not necessary to enumerate here the many passages in the novel in which the sertão appears as a concrete reality, be it through references to its physical, geographical aspects or through descriptions of its people's customs and way of life; however, it is pertinent to mention a few passages in which the term sertão is employed by the narrator in its referential sense of a certain, specific geographic region. Thus at the beginning of the novel, when referring to some people who are physically handicapped, Riobaldo says, "O sertão está cheio desses" (58), and later, describing a character from the sertão: "Se gordo próprio não era, isso só por no sertão não se ver nenhum homem gordo" (253). In the same way he affirms, in another passage, that "a vida vera é outra, do cidadão do sertão" (107), and remarks, regarding the jagunços' war: "Agora se ia gastar o tempo em guerras e guerras, morrendo e se matando, aos cinco, aos seis, aos dez, os homens todos mais valentes do sertão?" (342). The "catrumanos," a group of people who live in a kind of cave, isolated from everybody else in the area, are referred to as "groteiros dum sertão" (363), and the children who inhabit the region are "as infâncias deste sertão" (375). Finally, Riobaldo's great friend Diadorim, revealed at the end of the novel as a woman disguised as a man, is buried in a "campo do sertão" (564), and places such as Buruti-Comprido, Tamboril, Cambaúda, Virgens, Mata-Cachorro, das Cobras, etc., are referred to as "Em sertão são" (469).

These examples all indicate that the concept represented by the word sertão corresponds on one level in the mind of the narrator-protagonist to a concrete geographic region which is part of his life experience and constitutes the scenery around which he has accomplished his marches as a jagunço. Yet it is important to note that even in this sense the term cannot be understood as referring to a clearly delimited region, for it varies in the conception of the inhabitants of the area themselves. Hence Riobaldo's statement at the very beginning of the novel:

> O senhor tolere, isto é o sertão. Uns querem que não seja: que situado sertão é por os campos-gerais a fora a dentro, eles dizem, fim de rumo, terras altas, demais do Urucúia. Toleima. Para os de Corinto e do Curvelo, então, o aqui não é dito sertão? Ah, que tem maior! Lugar sertão se divulga: é onde os pastos carecem de fechos; onde um pode torar dez, quinze léguas, sem topar com casa de morador; e onde criminoso vive seu cristo-jesus, arredado do arrocho de autoridade. O Urucúia vem dos montões oestes. Mas, hoje, que na beira dele, tudo dá – fazendões de fazendas, almargem de vargens de bom render, as vazantes; culturas que vão de mata em mata, madeiras de grossura, até ainda virgens dessas lá há. O *gerais* corre em volta. Esses gerais são sem tamanho. Enfim, cada um o que quer aprova, o senhor sabe: pão ou pães, é questão de opiniães... O sertão está em toda a parte. (9)

The impossibility of tracing with precision the limits of the sertão is associated, in concrete terms, with the fact that it is not a uniform region but a vast expanse of territory, which differs in climate and vegetation from one part to another and whose great common denominator is the economic activity of cattle raising, to which critic Adonias Filho adds the miserable social condition of its inhabitants.[8] The sertão is indeed an agglomeration of several smaller regions that have been unified under a common label; this diversity is indicated in the book by the fact that the word is often employed in its plural form, *sertões,* and is sometimes followed by an adjective which specifies the place. Thus Riobaldo speaks of "as boiadas daqueles sertões" (382) and of a character who is a "rastreador, de todos esses sertões dos Gerais sabente" (302), and whenever he wants to specify a certain area, he says: "sertões da Jaíba" (175) or "sertão jequitinhão" (211).

The term *sertão,* still in its concrete sense, is also used to mean a region that is basically rural, as opposed to the city, here seen as a center of progress and of a more advanced civilization. It is in this

---

[8] Adonias Filho, "A ficção de Gimarães Rosa," in *Guimarães Rosa* (Lisbon: Instituto Luso-Brasileiro, 1969), pp. 11-22.

sense that Riobaldo once exclaims: "Ah, tempo de jagunço tinha mesmo de acabar, cidade acaba com o sertão. Acaba?" (159); and in another passage comments: "Sensato somente eu saísse do meio do sertão, is morar residido, em fazenda perto de cidade" (540). An area located far away from the big cities and having very little contact with them, the sertão present in *Grande sertão: veredas* is a kind of anachronic region that is in a stage of development not very different from that described in the reports made by voyagers throughout the colonial period. It is a land without law, a world of "absolute" men, "onde manda quem é forte, com as astúcias," a place where, as Riobaldo says, "Deus mesmo quando vier que venha armado" (20).

It is in this sense of the sertão that the main conflict of the novel on the factual, episodic level – the war that the jagunços wage first against the government soldiers and then, after Joca Ramiro's murder, against the traitors who killed him – can be understood. However, it is important to note that at this point the concept of the sertão as a physical region begins to be confused with that of a human reality, and the region which served the author as a point of departure comes to be represented by the system of values of the jagunço, here identified with the land: "Jagunço é o sertão" (294), says Riobaldo to his interlocutor, and his war, "o constante mexer do sertão" (341), is the weapon he wields to keep his world safe from the invasion of the city. The latter is the new, it is progress and civilization which enters the backlands in the form of its soldiers to conquer and civilize them; hence the reaction of the jagunços, by means of a war that is nothing but the social, economic, and cultural conflict of two societies that live side by side in considerably different stages of development.

This conflict between the old and the new, here represented by the sertão and the city, finds its best expression in the novel in the episode of Zé Bebelo's trial, an anthological passage that has been classified by Cavalcânti Proença in *Trilhas no Grande sertão*[9] as the dialogue between the sertão and the city. Zé Bebelo was a man who aspired to change the old habits of the sertão, to civilize it. He wanted to finish off the jagunços, "até o último, relimpar o

---

[9] Cavalcânti Proença, *Trilhas no Grande sertão* (Rio de Janeiro: Ministério da Educação e Cultura, 1958), p. 44.

mundo da jagunçada braba" (124), and after that to become a congressman with the purpose of building bridges, hospitals, factories, and schools in the sertão. He was a farmer who dreamed about big cities and his name in the newspapers and who, before marching against the sertão, learns to read and write and becomes an ally of soldiers and politicians. But he is captured by Joca Ramiro's group and submitted to a trial in which he is asked through the words of the leader: "Adianta querer saber muita coisa? O senhor sabia, lá para cima – me disseram. Mas, de repente, chegou neste sertão; viu tudo diverso diferente, o que nunca tinha visto. Sabença aprendida não adiantou para nada. Serviu algum?" (246-47). In the sertão it is of no use to be a learned man, and the great accusation against Zé Bebelo is that of being an outsider, of having attacked the land, for the purpose of changing its customs: "O senhor não é do sertão," says Joca Ramiro, "não é da terra.... O senhor veio querendo desnortear, desencaminhar os sertanejos de seu costume velho de lei" (247). And at the end of the trial Zé Bebelo is condemned to exile, a sentence perfectly appropriate to the kind of crime of which he is accused.

It is important to note, however, that this episode of Zé Bebelo's trial does not imply, as its sentence might indicate, a victory of the sertão over the city, for it contains the germs of the treason that will provoke the scission of the jagunço's group. It is true that Zé Bebelo is punished for his audacity in invading the sertão, and that the episode has had the effect of making him switch sides – for after Joca Ramiro's murder he returns with the firm intention of avenging him and becomes a jagunço chief – but by introducing the idea of a trial and obtaining a sentence that was different from death he has broken with the traditional habits o the sertão and has exposed it to the influence of the city. That is why the most conservative faction, here represented by the subleaders Hermógenes and Ricardão, having been beaten by the majority of the votes in the trial, rebelled against Joca Ramiro and decided to murder him.

On the level of events, which Proença calls the objective level of the narrative, Zé Bebelo's trial constitutes a turning point in the novel in the sense that it marks a borderline between two distinct moments of the jagunços' war: their fight against the government soldiers and their struggle for reunification after the split caused by the treason. However, in addition to this, the episode marks the introduction of new, civilizing habits into the backlands, a trend which will develop gradually, especially during the leadership first of Zé bebelo and then of Riobaldo. The consciousness of the changes they are introducing into the sertão makes these characters frequently hesitate in their decisions, fearful that they might be betraying their land. And in fact Zé Bebelo falls into this error, during the siege at the Tucano farm, by sending for the soldiers to counterattack Hermógenes, resulting in the loss of his leadership to Riobaldo.

But if both Zé Bebelo and Riobaldo introduce new customs into the sertão, a distinction must be made between them. Zé Bebelo has never been a real man from the sertão, in that he has never identified with the soil, has never totally adapted to the way of life characteristic of the land. His aim was to change this way of life, to break with the established order, and he does not hesitate to march against the sertão, consciously at first, when fighting the jagunços, and unconsciously, perhaps later, when sending for the goverment politicians to interfere in a internal affair. Zé Bebelo comes and goes to and from the sertão throughout the novel, and at the end, when Riobaldo sees him for the last time, his plans are to settle down in a big city, for, as the narrator registers, "a água e o chão [do sertão] não queriam saber dele" (293). Riobaldo, on the contrary, is a man from the sertão, an individual so much integrated with his region that the latter exerts upon him a kind of fatalistic influence from which he cannot escape: "Sertão é isto," he says, "o senhor empurra para trás, mas de repente ele volta a rodear o senhor dos lados. Sertão é quando menos se espera" (271).

It is this integration of Riobaldo with the sertão, his identification with the land and what it represents, that makes him successful in precisely those aspects in which his predecessors had failed. A son of the sertão, Riobaldo is aware that "a gente só sai do sertão é tomando contra dele a dentro" (264), for, as he tells his interlocutor, "o sertão não tem janelas nem portas. E a regra é assim: ou o senhor bendito governa o sertão, ou o sertão maldito vos governa" (466). But governing the sertão paradoxically implies obeying it, accepting the duties imposed by circumstances. This is what Riobaldo means when he states, "Rebulir com o sertão, como dono? Mas o sertão era para, aos poucos, se ir obedecendo a ele; não era para à força se compor. Todos que malmontam no sertão só alcançam de reger em rédea por uns trechos, que sorrateiro o sertão vai virando tigre por baixo da sela" (354). Zé Bebelo, an outsider, had not been able to understand the sertão, for he always approached it from his own perspective; he failed as a result of having attempted to impose his own values upon it. Riobaldo, though hesitant at the beginning, eventually learns how to listen to the call of the land, and is successful only insofar as he has been able to identify with it and to assume such an identity up to the end. But his success, like everything else in the novel, has a double meaning, for in order to achieve such a stage he has had to submit to the fatalistic power of the milieu and accept a destiny that seemed to have been traced for him beforehand. Hence his confession, which sounds like a lament: "O sertão me produz, depois me engoliu, depois me cuspiu do quente da boca" (550).

This double character of Riobaldo's achievement, which is part of the general theme of the relativity and reversibility of things present throughout the novel, is significant also on the level of events, in that it establishes a distinction between the conflict of sertão vs. city which we have been discussing here and the dichotomy found in earlier Latin American fiction, which inevitably results in man's final ruin or destruction. Such a distinction is a consequence of the fact that whereas in that older type of fiction nature or the countryside (be it the sertão, the jungles, or the plains) is always seen, from a one-sided perspective, as a victim of man's ambition and civilizing purposes, which therefore must be punished at any cost, the sertão in *Grande sertão: veredas* is an ambiguous reality, endowed simultaneously with the attributes of a mother and those of an enemy which, as Riobaldo himself states, "ajuda, com enorme poder, ou é traiçoeiro, muito desastroso" (501). The sertão is not in Rosa's work a mere antagonist of man, as in the famous cycle of the jungle novel in which barbarism vs. civilization constituted a central element, but rather a multiple, complex, and ambiguous region, constructed under a plural semantic axis which oscillates according to man's way of relating to it. This is the meaning of the words of the old man of whom Riobaldo inquires about the nature of the sertão: "Sertão não é malino nem caridoso, mano oh mano! –... ele tira ou dá, ou agrada ou amarga, ao senhor, conforme o senhor mesmo" (490).

But this notion of the sertão as a multiple, ambiguous region where, as Riobaldo says, "tem de tudo" (497), and where the most contradictory elements, such as "confusão" ("confusion"), "sossego" ("peace"), and above all "Deus" ("God") and the "Demo" ("Devil"), coexist in constant tension, places us face to face with another reality, of a wider scope, that transcends the region in the sense in which we have been discussing it up to the present. *Sertão*, at this point, is no longer a geographical reality that can be characterized by either its physical or its social or economic aspects, but rather a microcosm of the world, a mysterious, unlimited region in which man lives in constant search for meaning. Hence Riobaldo's remark to his interlocutor: "Eu queria decifrar as coisas que são importantes," and later, "Lhe falo do sertão, do que não sei. Um grande sertão! Não sei. Ninguém ainda não sabe. Só umas raríssimas pessoas – e só, essas poucas veredas, veredazinhas" (96-97). In this universal region, which has been compared by critics to the Chekhovian steppes, Cervantes' La Mancha, or even Joyce's Dublin, the jagunço lives with all his contradictions, and faces – in his status as a "provisory" man – a series of situations that are nothing but a representation of everyone's daily life, especially in its extreme moments of tension. This is the reason Antônio Cândido has affirmed that the sertão is the world and the jagunços are all of us,[10] a statement that can easily be corroborated if we think of Riobaldo's words: "O sertão é do tamanho do mundo" (71), "Sertão é o sozinho.... Sertão: é dentro da gente" (292-93), or yet, "A minha terra era longe dali, no restante do mundo. O sertão é sem lugar" (334).

This sense of the sertão as a microcosm of the world is that which predominates on the subjective level of the narrative, constituted by Riobaldo's inner conflicts and metaphysical quest, for – as we have seen when discussing the protagonist's status as a jagunço – both these conflicts and his quest for the meaning of life are universal preoccupations that transcend the barriers of a specific geographical region. If this affirmation leaves no doubt regarding the character's metaphysical quest, it is, however, worthwhile to stress that his inner conflicts, rather than being exclusive to the type he embodies – the jagunço – are existential conflicts common to all men at all times. It is true that these conflicts cannot be totally dissociated from the circumstances of his life –

---

[10] Antônio Cândido, "O homem dos avessos," *Tese e antítese* (São Paulo: Companhia Editora Nacional, 1964), pp. 119-40. Cited henceforth as *TA*.

for example, his being a man from the sertão who admired the jagunço's way of life brought about the question of his being a jagunço, and his ability as such raised the question of his becoming a leader – but to consider them as specific for this reason is certainly to go beyond the point. Riobaldo's conflicts on this subjective level – his hesitation between spiritual love for his pure Otacília and carnal desire for the prostitute Nhorinhá; his insecurity resulting from the simultaneous attraction and repulsion he feels toward his friend Diadorim, who embodies, through his androgyny, both the licit and the illicit sides of love; his wish to carry out that which he sees as his duty and at the same time his fear of doing it – are all universal conflicts with which man has to deal in the world.

This notion of the sertão as a universal region is made even more evident in the novel through the theme of the voyage, represented by the word "travessia" ("crossing, passage through"), repeated often throughout the narrative. If on the denotative level the word certainly refers to Riobaldo's crossing of the sertão, to his marches and countermarches in defense of the jagunços' cause, it indicates on the connotative or symbolic level the life-journey which the protagonist takes in his search for the meaning of things and the essence of the human condition. It is in this double, ambiguous sense of a voyage through the sertão at the same time as a specific geographical region and as a representation of the world that the term is employed in the following passages: "Aparecia que nós dois [Diadorim and the narrator] já estávamos cavalhando lado a lado, par-a-par, a vai-a-vida inteira. Que: coragem é o que o coração bate; se não bate falso. Travessia – do sertão – a toda travessia" (473) and

> Sertão velho de idades. Porque serra pede serra – e dessas, altas, é que o senhor vê bem: como é que o sertão vem e volta. Não adianta se dar as costas. Ele beira aqui, e vai beirar outros lugares, tão distantes. Rumor dele se escuta. Sertão sendo do sol e dos pássaros: urubu, gavião – que sempre voam, às imensidões, por sobre... Travessia perigosa, mas é a da vida. Sertão que se alteia e se abaixa. Mas que as curvas dos campos estendem sempre para mais longe. Ali envelhece vento. E os brabos bichos, do fundo dele. (510)

In the novel life is a crossing, a journey to knowledge, a process of learning that stops only at the moment of one's death, and every step each man undertakes along his way is a moment of risk which places him face to face with mystery, with the unknown. Hence Riobaldo's maxim "Viver é muito perigoso," ("Living is very dangerous,") also repeated frequently. Man begins from nothing, from a pure state of innocence – "nonada" – and attains knowledge through his experiences, for as the narrator says, "aprender-a-viver é que é o viver, mesmo" (550), but since both he and the world are dynamic realities, his achievements are always provisory, and what characterizes him is an indefatigable state of search. Hence the statement, "Vivendo se aprende; mas o que se aprende, mais, é só a fazer outras maiores perguntas" (389-90).

It is important to note that at this point we can no longer separate Riobaldo's life from the narration he makes to his interlocutor: the existential itinerary which he follows is not concluded in the past; it is an ongoing process that continues throughout the narrative. Hence his statement, "Estou contando não é uma vida de sertanejo, seja se for jagunço, mas a matéria vertente. Queria entender do medo e da coragem, e da gã que empurra a gente para fazer tantos atos, dar corpo ao suceder" (96). The protagonist's experiences as a jagunço, his battles and toils in the backlands, as well as the inner conflicts he had at that time, are simply the first part of a voyage which goes on into the present, and these elements are important only insofar as they are still alive within him, as they have left marks in the form of questions which trouble him now. These questions – the *matéria vertente* – form the substance of his narration, which, far from being a cold report of past facts and events, is a living process, a phase of his search process which develops and takes shape through words in the very act of narration. That is why the whole novel is constructed in the form of a question which extends far beyond the possibility of any sort of answer. The protagonist had the experiences which he is presently narrating, but in the narration he experiences them again, for his narration is, in sum, an effort to decipher what he has not yet been able to understand. This is what Riobaldo means when he says to his interlocutor: "Conto ao senhor é o que eu sei e o senhor não sabe, mas principal quero contar é o que eu não sei se sei, e que pode ser que o senhor saiba" (217).

In this sense, the "travessia" that Riobaldo undergoes in the novel embraces yet another meaning – that of a voyage through words, through literature – and only at this point can the role of the interlocutor be seen in its full extent. For this character, often described as a learned man, "com toda leitura e suma doutoração" (15), has come to the sertão "devassar a raso este mar de territórios para sortimento de conferir o que existe" (26), but when he meets Riobaldo on his farm the physical itinerary which he had planned for himself is replaced by the latter's report and transformed into an imaginary journey – a journey through art. Thus, rather than coming to know the sertão merely in its physical, external aspects, he becomes acquainted with it through the experience of one of its men, and sees it then as a human region, re-created through art. That is why the novel begins with the word *nonada* ("nonothing"), forming a sentence by itself, and ends with the word *travessia*, also employed under the same circumstances, followed by the symbol of infinity. Riobaldo's interlocutor is the first link of a chain, a representative of the reader, and the entire novel is a journey that every reader will take from the moment he opens the book until he closes it. And since the reader is an active participant in this journey, who is urged to think, to meditate upon the facts narrated, and even to make conclusions about them – "O senhor pense, o senhor ache. O senhor ponha enredo" (292), Riobaldo urges – it is integrated into his own existential itinerary and becomes, as in the narrator's case, a part of his life. Thus the sertão is revealed to him not only as a representation of the world but also as an artistic region that is transformed into a part of his own life experience. It is a living reality, revived every time he travels through the book's pages.

This view of the sertão as a multiple, ambiguous reality, simultaneously specific and generic, concrete and abstract, external and internal, distinguishes the region represented in *Grande sertão: veredas* from that encountered in the earlier regionalist fiction in Latin America. Whereas in this type of fiction the region is seen only from a one-sided perspective, either as a picturesque natural refuge or as an inhospitable land that engulfs and destroys man, and is always portrayed, with a series of clichés, in its superficial aspects alone, in Rosa's novel it is a living, dynamic reality, deep and contradictory, made known to the reader through the view and life experience of a man who carries it in his veins. The sertão in

Grande sertão: veredas is certainly also the representation of a region in its typical aspects, as we have seen when discussing the referential side of the sign, but, since these aspects are always focused on from the point of view of man's relation to them, rather than in and by themselves alone, and since man constitutes the pivotal element in the novel, it transcends the limits of the region and is projected into a wider, universal scope.

3. The Dimensions of Reality in *Grande Sertão: Veredas*

> Se descreves o mundo tal qual é, não haverá em tuas palavras senão muitas mentiras e nenhuma verdade.
>
> Leo Tolstoy

> Sem fantasia teremos um mundo de fatos, situações e acontecimentos, mas não uma realidade.
>
> Ernst Fischer

> O diabo não existe, por isso ele é também tão forte.
>
> Brazilian backlands proverb

3.1. *The Logos and the Mythos*

The neutralization of the second opposition about which we are concerned here — objective realism vs. other levels of reality — will also be studied in this section in relation to the same two elements of fiction around which we have centered our discussion on the opposition between regionalism and universalism, that is, our protagonist, Riobaldo, and his environment, the sertão. However, since the point of view of the narrative is that of the first person and the sertão is made known to the reader through the consciousness of the narrator-protagonist, we will focus on the former briefly at first, and then concentrate on the latter, without losing track, of course, of the relationship existing between the two elements, which cannot be dissociated.

We have seen in the first section that the kind of realism that has always been present in Latin American literature has very little to do with the "realism of facts" that dominated the European literary scene during the second half of the nineteenth century. This kind of objectivist realism, based on an empiricist view of reality, entered Latin America as a result of French influence upon the continent and played an important role in the formation of the so-called socially committed current of the novel. But in spite of the significance of this type of novel within the continent's literary panorama, there has never been an identification between the world view expressed by it and the spirit of the people and their cultural tradition. Latin America is, the authors of the "new narrative" affirm, a land of extreme contrasts, a place where the most extraordinary events occur every day and constitute a natural aspect of people's daily life; thus it cannot be fully represented when seen from a purely rationalistic perspective.

Although the consciousness of this fact on the part of the writers of Latin America's "new narrative" has come about only as a result of a general tendency against objective realism existing in twentieth-century Western literature, the idea that reality must be represented from the point of view of as many aspects as possible has become an imperative in the continent's letters, and they have not hesitated to defend such a position both in manifestos and in interviews they have given. The cultural reality of Latin America is magical, these authors affirm, in the sense that it does not fit into the parameters established by rationalistic logic; therefore it must be represented in an appropriate manner. The rationalistic view of reality is a certain European way of approaching things, an imported view not at all suited to represent the world of the New Land, a world where, as Carpentier stated in *El reino de este mundo*, "Todavía no se ha terminado de establecer, por ejemplo, un recuento de cosmogonías" (p. 2).

A man from the Brazilian backlands, a region characterized essentially by mystery and the unknown, where powerful farmers and influential politicians live side by side with jagunços and with people like the "catrumanos," almost a remnant of the cave man, Guimarães Rosa is not an exception among the contemporary Latin American writers who rebel against the tyranny of rationalism. In an interview with the German critic Günter Lorenz he declared, after making it clear that to understand the Brazilian way of life it is important above all to learn that knowlege is different from logic, "Espero una literatura tan ilógica como la mía, que transforme el mundo en un Sertão, en el cual la única realidad es lo increíble," and adds that *Grande sertão: veredas* is "mi autobiografía irracional."[11]

That the sertão represented in *Grande sertão: veredas* is an illogical world in the sense that it is constructed within a sphere which transcends the barriers imposed by rationalistic thought is made evident in the novel by those elements that form the mental complex of the people who inhabit the region, namely their mysticism, their beliefs and superstitions, and their way of relating to one another and to external facts or events. Although is seems irrelevant to enumerate these elements here, or even to discuss them separately since they form the atmosphere which pervades the entire novel, it is worth mentioning that they range from mere superstitions and premonitions to belief in apparitions and devotion to healers and fortune tellers. The most significant of these elements, in that it constitutes one of the major themes of the novel, is the fear of the devil, a being that is present in its absence, "que não há, havendo," as Riobaldo frequently remarks.

The sertão which forms the universe of the novel is a melting pot reflecting the process of acculturation characteristic of the Latin American continent; it is a land where different people live with their customs and habits, their religions and myths, and where these different elements are all mixed together into a kind of syncretism whose major trait is perhaps a belief in the supernatural. In such a universe, which has been defined by critics as magical or "maravilloso," to use Carpentier's term, the existence of the devil is a constant threat that haunts people from their early childhood; it is not strange, then, that this preoccupation is at the core of Riobaldo's narrative. Belief in the devil as an external entity is a part of that world, and the respect it inspires takes the form of a mythical terror that may exert a strong influence upon the actions of people. Thus at the very beginning of the narrative there is a reference to a man, José Simplício, who is said to have a little devil in his house, "miúdo satananzim, preso obrigado a ajudar em toda ganância que executa; razão que o Simplício se empresa em vias de completar de rico" (10), and the jagunço Hermógenes, antagonist of Riobaldo, is frequently referred to by several characters as having once made a pact with the devil: "O Hermógenes tem pauta... Ele se quis com o Capiroto" (47), says João Bugre, one

---

[11] Günter Lorenz, "Diálogo con Guimarães Rosa," *Mundo Nuevo*, March 1970, pp. 45-46.

of Riobaldo's companions, and later Lacrau, another jagunço, declares, "O Hermógenes era positivo pactário.... Pra matar, ele foi sempre muito pontual... Se diz. O que é porque o Cujo rebatizou a cabeça dele com sangue certo: que foi o de um homen são e justo, sangrado sem razão" (385).

Having come from this world where people avoid pronouncing the name of the devil for fear he may appear, where a jagunço repents of his crimes in the middle of a combat exclaiming that he has seen the Virgin, where a young lady is believed to have become a miracle-worker after having fasted for three days in a row, and where the phenomenon of *ignis fatuus* is interpreted as a divine punishment, Riobaldo cannot help also being a believer in these things, an individual who certainly possesses a mythical-sacred consciousness; this is made evident at several different moments of the narrative. Thus when the jagunço João Goanhá affirms that Hermógenes has contracted a pact with the devil and the latter acts in his place, Riobaldo confesses his belief by remarking: "Nisso todos acreditavam. Pela fraqueza do meu medo e pela força do meu ódio, acho que eu fui o primeiro que cri" (64); and in the middle of the final battle he declares that he has seen Hermógenes as an embodiment of the devil: "E mesmo me alembro do que se deu, por mim: que eu estava crente, forte, que, do demo, do Cão, sem açamo, quem era era ele – o Hermógenes!" (520). But Hermógenes is not the only character in the narrative that Riobaldo identifies with the Spirit of Evil; thus in another passage the protagonist kills a man, Treciziano, believing that he was fighting and killing the devil:

> O que houve, que se deu. Que vi. Com a sede sofrida, um incha, padece nas vistas, chega fica cego. Mas vi. Foi num átimo. Como que por distraído: num dividido de minuto, a gente perde o tino por dez anos. Vi: ele – o chapéu que não quebrava bem, o punhal que sobressaía muito na cintura, o monho, o mudar das caras... Ele era o demo, de mim diante... O Demo! Fez uma careta, que sei que brilhava. Era o Demo, por escarnir, próprio pessoal ... Cortei por cima do adão... Ele Outro caiu do cavalo, já veio antes do chão com os olhos duros apagados... Morreu maldito, morreu com a goela roncando na garganta! (482)

Owing to these beliefs, to his mythical-sacred consciousness, Riobaldo himself decides to contract a pact with the devil, an episode which can be seen as crucial in relation to the entire narrative; when he reaches the Coruja, he recognizes the "lugar demarcado, começo de um grande penar em grandes pecados terríveis" and observes: "Agouro? Eu creio no temor de certos pontos. Tem, onde o senhor encontra a palma da mão em terra, e sua mão treme pra trás ou é a terra que treme se abaixando. . . . Ali eu tive limite certo" (379).

However, at this point it is important to state that if Riobaldo undoubtedly possesses a mythical-sacred consciousness, as we can see from the above examples, it is not this aspect of his personality alone that characterizes his Weltanschauung, for he also has a logical-rational mind, resulting perhaps from having received some formal education, which runs counter to his mythical consciousness and forces him to question his own values as a man from the sertão. The coexistence in the mind of the narrator-protagonist of these two mental structures, apparently irreconcilable but whose fusion characterizes exactly comtemporary Latin American man, sets the basic conflict which forms the core of the narrative of *Grande sertão: veredas* – namely the conflict between the *mythos* and the *logos*. Riobaldo is a man divided between two worlds, one of a mythical-sacred character and the other based on a logical-rational view,[12] and his conflict is the consequence of a desperate search for identity that can be resolved only in a dialectical synthesis which consists of the fusion of the two opposing elements.

The logical-rational side of Riobaldo's consciousness is reflected in the novel every time he places himself in a critical position in relation to those aspects which characterize the mythical-sacred consciousness of the man from the sertão. For example, at the very beginning of the narrative when, after reporting to his interlocutor the episode of the calf which people believed was the devil, he exclaims: "Povo prascóvio" (9); or later when, having narrated the episode of the *ignis fatuus*, he comments about the people: "Querem-porque-querem inventar maravilhas glorionhas, depois eles mesmos acabam crendo e temendo" (72). But this side of his consciousness is above all revealed through the necessity Riobaldo

---

[12] The terms *mítico-sacral* 'mythical-sacred' and *lógico-racional* 'logical-rational' have been employed by José Hildebrando Dacanal in his "A epopéia Riobaldiana," in *Nova narrativa épica no Brasil* (Porto Alegre: Livraria Sulina Editora, 1973), pp. 7-108.

constantly feels for denying the existence of the devil. It is this logical-rational component of his mind that compels him to tell his story to his interlocutor – an educated urban citizen – in the hope that he will confirm the nonexistence of the entity. However, the very necessity of insisting upon the issue and of searching for someone else's help to support his point indicates the hesitation of the character and his oscillation between two worlds.

Riobaldo's conflict about believing or not believing in the existence of the devil, or rather his oscillation between the mythical-sacred world of the sertão and the logical-rational world of his interlocutor, finds its best expression in the episode of the pact, in which the narrator decides to face the forces he feared in order to be able to assume a position of leadership and accomplish the vengeance for which the jagunços were striving. This episode, a decisive moment in Riobaldo's existential itinerary since it marks a change in his behavior that makes possible the achievement of his goal, is also one of the most ambiguous passages in the novel. While on the one hand it is narrated from a naive perspective, with no critical detachment whatsoever, on the other it does not contain any element that might exclude the possibility of a rationalistic interpretation. Riobaldo goes to meet the devil at a certain crossroad one midnight and invokes him several times, but the latter does not show up as an external entity. The protagonist insists on calling him for some time and finally concludes:

> E foi aí. Ele não existe, e não apareceu nem respondeu – que é um falso imaginado. Mas eu supri que ele tinha me ouvido. Me ouviu, a conforme a ciência da noite e o envir de espaços, que medeia. Como que adquirisse minhas palavras todas; fechou o arrocho do assunto. Ao que eu recebi de volta um adejo, um gozo de agarro, daí umas tranqüilidades – de pancada. Lembrei dum rio que viesse adentro a casa de meu pai. Vi as asas. Arquei o puxo do poder meu, naquele átimo. Aí podia ser mais? A peta, eu querer saldar: que isso não é falável. As coisas assim a gente mesmo não pega nem abarca. Cabem é no brilho da noite. Aragem do sagrado. Absolutas estrelas! (398)

Although it is clear in the passage that the devil has not appeared as an external entity, Riobaldo does not reject the idea that he may have been present in his absence: "... eu supri que ele tinha me ouvido. Me ouviu, a conforme a ciência da noite e o envir de espaços, que medeia," and registers that he has gone through a transformation that will later be manifested by means of his own actions as a jagunço and leader of his group. Thus, if on the one hand the episode can be interpreted in rationalistic terms as a consciousness awakening on the part of the protagonist to the evil that lies within himself and an acceptance of it that marks his evolution from a Manicheist perspective to a multiple view of reality based on the contradictory character of human beings, on the other it does not exclude the possibility of a magical interpretation, which will continue to be present in Riobaldo's mind through the fear that will torment him henceforth that he has sold his soul to the devil. Because of this fear he will devote the rest of his life after attaining vengeance to religious practices; will make statements such as: "O que devia de haver, era de se reunirem-se os sábios, políticos, constituições gradas, fecharem o definitivo a noção – proclamar por uma vez, artes assembléias, que não tem diabo nenhum, não existe, não pode. Valor de lei! Só assim, davam tranqüilidade boa à gente" (16); and will finally narrate his life to his interlocutor. Riobaldo wants to be sure whether the pact has been contracted or not, and at the end he seems inclined to deny its existence, but his doubt is never completely abolished, as is indicated both by the answer he receives from Compadre Quelemém – the first one to whom he reported his story, who says, "Comprar ou vender, às vezes, são as ações que são as quase iguais" (571) – and by the final paragraph of the book, essentially ambiguous: "Amável o senhor me ouviu, minha idéia confirmou: que o Diabo não existe. Pois não? O senhor é homem soberano, circunspecto. Amigos somos. Nonada. O diabo não há! É o que eu digo, se for... Existe é homem humano. Travessia" (571).

This ambiguity of the narrative of *Grande sertão: veredas* has led Antônio Cândido to write in his essay "O sertão e o mundo" of the presence in the novel of an "atmosfera reversível, onde se cortam o mágico e o lógico," and another critic, Roberto Schwarz, in his study *"Grande sertão e Dr. Faustus,"* of the existence in Rosa's book of the myth "com ressalvas."[13] While myth is unquestionably present in every aspect of *Grande sertão: veredas* to the point of

---

[13] Antônio Cândido, "O sertão o mundo," *Diálogo* [São Paulo], 8 (Nov. 1957), 16; Roberto Schwarz, *"Grande sertão e Dr. Faustus,"* in *A sereia e o desconfiado: ensaios críticos* (Rio de Janeiro: Civilização Brasileira, 1965), p. 29.

constituting one of the basic elements of the entire narrative (it is, as we have seen, at the basis of Riobaldo's conflict), at no moment it acquires autonomy and is never seen as independent from man's view of the world. On the contrary, it is always focused upon as a product of man's relationship with the world, a product of human interpretation, and therefore as an element of the culture represented in the novel. The *mythos* in Rosa's book is not an element per se, but a part of the mental complex of the men from the sertão, and as such it does not exclude the *logos*, by infringing the laws of verisimilitude. The two elements, the *mythos* and the *logos*, far from being exclusive, as in the traditional novel, are here the two sides of the same coin that complement each other.

This integration of the *mythos* and the *logos* is even better achieved in the novel thanks to the kind of narrator selected to report the events. For, being a character divided between two worlds of different origins, Riobaldo expresses through his discourse the doubts and oscillation which disturb him. Thus, if on the one hand he narrates the mythical episodes from a naive perspective, in the same manner in which an objective event is told (see, for example, the episode of the pact as contrasted with the judgment of Zé Bebelo), on the other he raises through his questioning a series of doubts regarding their truthfulness, and this situation of uncertainty is transmitted to the reader. The narrator questions the domain of rationalism, by calling attention to myth, but by also questioning its existence, he does not eliminate the possibility of a rationalistic perspective and reveals a world view that represents in its multiplicity the reality of contemporary Latin American man. This is what the critic Suzi Frankl Sperber intends to express in her study *Caos e cosmos: leituras de Guimarães Rosa,* when she affirms that "para o Guimarães Rosa de *Grande sertão: veredas,* a realidade única é a resultante de uma dialética, dialética que se resolve afinal na unidade das duas entidades contrárias."[14]

---

[14] Suzi Frankl Sperber, *Caos e cosmos: leituras de Guimarães Rosa* (São Paulo: Duas Cidades, 1976), pp. 120-21.

3.2. The Ambiguity of Diadorim

We have seen so far how the opposition between objective realism and other levels of reality or, more specifically here, between rationalism and irrationalism or logic and illogic, is neutralized in *Grande sertão: veredas* as a result of the conflict within the narrator-protagonist, a conflict deriving from his polarity between two opposing world views – one of a mythical-sacred origin, typical of the men from the sertão, and the other of a logical-rational quality, characteristic of Western man in general – and of the treatment given to that conflict, which is revealed in its dynamics or rather in its own process of development. However, this conflict, which in the text itself takes the form of a question about the existence or nonexistence of the devil, is not an isolated element in the narrative and the neutralization it effects of the traditional oppositions so dominant in the earlier Latin American novel is also present in other elements that are directly associated with it. We will therefore take a look now at some of these elements, such as Riobaldo's ambiguous friendship for his companion Diadorim and the role played by chance in the course of his life.

With regard to the first of these elements, let us consider the words of Antônio Cândido in "O sertão e o mundo":

> A amizade ambígua por Diadorim aparece como primeiro e decisivo elemento que desloca o narrador do seu centro de gravidade. Levado a ele (ou ela) por um instinto poderoso que reluta em confessar a si próprio, e ao mesmo tempo tolhido pela aparência masculina, Riobaldo tergiversa e admite na personalidade um fator de desnorteio, que facilita a eclosão de sentimentos e comportamentos estranhos, cuja possibilidade se insinua pela narrativa e o vai lentamente preparando para ações excepcionais, ao obliterar as fronteiras entre lícito e ilícito. (P. 16)

The above statement indicates the basic points present in the motif of Riobaldo's friendship with Diadorim which account for the neutralzation of the opposition we have been discussing; we will consider these points separately now and start by tracing the development of the conflict responsible for disorienting the narrator's personality and consequently leading to his pact with the devil.

The seeds of this conflict, which is one of the central elements of the entire narrative, are present in the report of the secene in which Riobaldo, still an adolescent, becomes acquainted with Diadorim, on the banks of the de-Janeiro river, an affluent of the São Francisco. In this episode, of a highly lyrical tone, the fascination exerted by Diadorim upon the protagonist is expressed by the way in which he is described and by the narration of a series of incidents that reveal his courage and strength of character. The boy was "muito diferente," the narrator states, "gostei daquelas finas feições, a voz mesma, muito leve, muito aprazível. Porque ele falava sem mudança, nem intenção, sem sobejo de esforço, fazia de conversar uma conversinha adulta e antiga" (99), and later adds: "Ele, o menino, era dessemelhante, já disse, não dava minúcia de pessoa outra nenhuma. Comparável um suave de ser, mas asseado e forte – assim se fosse um cheiro bom sem cheiro nenhum sensível.... A bem dizer, ele pouco falasse. Se via que estava apreciando o ar do tempo, calado e sabido, e tudo nele era segurança em si" (100). This boy, presented through the eyes of Riobaldo as a delicate yet secure person, capable of extremely courageous actions, who teaches him a maxim that will become one of the basic goals of his life, "Carece de ter coragem" (102), induces him to take a risky canoe ride up to the confluence of the São Francisco and the de-Janeiro. At the end of this episode, characterized in its entirety by the symbolism of water and seen by several critics as a kind of ritual of initiation, the protagonist's transformation is registered as follows: "O sério é isto, da estória toda – por isso foi que a estória eu lhe contei –: eu não sentia nada. Só uma transformação, pesável. Muita coisa importante falta nome" (105).

The fascination exerted by the young man upon Riobaldo and the transformation it effected in him are stressed at their second meeting, now adults, in which the protagonist decides to join Joca Ramiro's group, having realized that he could no longer dispense with the company of Diadorim. Riobaldo was at that moment fleeing from Zé Bebelo's group, but after the meeting with Diadorim, which happened "sem o razoável comum, sobrefalseado, como do que só em jornal e livro é que se lê" (133), he declares: "Eu não podia mais, por meu próprio querer, ir me separar da companhia dele, por lei nenhuma; podia? O que eu entendi em mim: direito como se, no reencontrando aquela hora aquele Menino-Moço, eu tivesse acertado de encontrar, para o todo sempre, as regências de uma alguma a minha família" (134).

Although the ambiguity of Riobaldo's feelings towards Diadorim is not yet conscious by the time of this second meeting, the above statement about the dominion the latter exerts upon him as a consequence of his fascination indicates the existence of a conflict, confirmed by the need Riobaldo feels to explain to his interlocutor: "De seguir assim, sem a dura decisão, feito cachorro magro que espera viajantes em ponto de rancho, o senhor quem sabe vá achar que eu seja homem sem caráter. Eu mesmo pensei. Conheci que estava chocho, dado no mundo, vazio de um meu dever honesto. Tudo, naquele tempo, e de cada banda que eu fosse, eram pessoas matando e morrendo, vivendo numa fúria firme, numa certeza, e eu não pertencia a razão nenhuma, não guardava fé e nem fazia parte" (135-36). A man from the sertão who admires courage and strength of will, Riobaldo does not accept the idea of submitting to his friend, but since he cannot escape from the latter's dominion, he sees this as a weakness on his part and suffers as a result of his incapacity to react. By this time the character is already divided, oscillating between an unexplainable attraction to his friend and a simultaneous, yet unsuccessful, effort to resist such an attraction; this polarity is the first stage of a conflict which will be developed later.

This conflict, of a moral character, is intensified during the period in which Riobaldo, having joined Joca Ramiro's group, is placed in daily contact with Diadorim. In this period, marked by the roughness of the jagunço's life, the presence of his friend constitutes a kind of oasis, a peaceful and joyful recess, and Riobaldo is drawn closer and closer to him. At Diadorim's side, Riobaldo learns how to appreciate every aspect of nature: "Diadorim me pôs o rastro dele para sempre em todas essas quisquilhas da natureza" (29), and he is brought to see the positive side of life, but the intuition that there is someting in their relationship which runs counter to his moral principles gives him a feeling of repulsion that functions as an opposing force. This oscillating movement of attraction and repulsion brings him into a process of constant questioning about the nature of his feelings which leads to a revelation in the episode of the Guararavacã do Guaicuí. In this place, whose name he repeats several times to his interlocutor, as if to register it forever, Riobaldo finally discovers that he "gostava de Diadorim – de amor mesmo amor, mal encoberto em amizade" (274).

At this moment, the inner conflict of the character, which so far had been limited to a preconscious level, rather than finding its solution enters its most intense phase. Riobaldo sees as absurd the idea of his loving another man and constantly asks himself: "De que jeito eu podia amar um homem, meu de natureza igual, macho em suas roupas e suas armas, espalhado rústico em suas ações?!" (466), but the realization that he could not deny such a feeling or even escape from its attraction drives him into a real torment which disorients him completely. From now on, his oscillation becomes increasingly frequent, and the gap already existing between his will and his acts is made much more significant. Several times he attempts to abandon the jagunço's life and establish himself far away from Diadorim, but the latter's power over him is so strong that he eventually not only submits to it but also makes his feeling the principal motivation for his actions. As a consequence of this he commits himself to the jagunços' cause, for, as he declared when he discovered that Joca Ramiro was Diadorim's father, "pelo nome de seu pai, Joca Ramiro, eu agora matava e morria, se bem" (40) and he will seek courage and strength by contracting the pact with the devil.

This dilemma in which the character finds himself, resolved only at the end of the narrative, after the death of Diadorim, by the revelation of the latter's true sex, leads Riobaldo several times to identify his feeling with and evil force, an act of the devil. Thus, in the following passage, when comparing his love for his companion with that he nourishes for Otacília, the girl to whom he becomes engaged, he says: "Se um aquele amor veio de Deus, como veio, então – o outro? ... Todo tormento" (134). But at this point it is important to note that this identification, far from endowing his feeling with any sort of magical power, simply serves to stress the duality of the protagonist – a man, as we have seen, divided between a mythical-sacred and a logical-rational world. If on the one hand Riobaldo may submit to the call of his feeling, which seems to him a supernatural force, on the other the restlessness expressed through his questioning indicates that he does not completely believe in the supernatural character of this force, and that his attribution of such a quality to it may simply be a way of providing an explanation for something which he cannot rationally apprehend or control. This is what the critic Benedito Nunes, who has studied the subject in an essay entitled "Guimarães Rosa," means when he says that what Riobaldo calls "feitiço, artes e partes do Demo, astúcias do Maligno,... [provém] menos de uma potência estranha, exterior ao homem, do que dos excessos, das 'demasias do coração.'"[15]

These "excessos" or "demasias do coração" to which Nunes refers are the irrational elements that man cannot understand or control, and it is common, especially among the predominantly mythical-sacred cultures, to identify these elements with supernatural forces. However, since Riobaldo is not exclusively a man from the sertão, but also one who has assimilated the values and world view of a logical-rational culture, his situation is once again ambiguous and the character is put into a kind of impasse: on the one hand, he wants to accept the state of things based on the idea that it might have been caused by some kind of magical power against which it is unthinkable to react, but on the other he cannot admit this explanation and sees his conformity to it as an error for which he is to blame.

The impasse into which the character is brought indicates per se a neutralization of the opposition between objective realism and other levels of reality, owing to the fact that both the magical and the rational possibilities are placed on the same level. However, such a neutralization is made even more significant in the novel when we think of another element, of primary importance here: Riobaldo's ambiguity has an objective counterpart in the corpus of the narrative in the figure of Diadorim, who embodies in his own being all the contradictory elements of human nature. The presence of this androgynous character, always portrayed in his contrasting aspects as one who "suspirava de ódio como se fosse por amor" (30), or who "não largava o fogo de gelo daquela idéia" (32), and who is referred to by Riobaldo as "a minha neblina" (25), is a fundamental element at this point of our discussion, because

---

[15] Benedito Nunes, "Guimarães Rosa," *O dorso do tigre* (São Paulo: Perspectiva, 1969), p. 144.

it places the protagonist's conflict out of a sphere of pure subjectivism and introduces by these means a general questioning about the nature of reality.

Having also fallen in love with Riobaldo from the very beginning of her companionship with him, Diadorim has always acted in an ambiguous manner in relation to him and consequently has, if not provoked, at least strongly contributed to the development of his conflict. Diadorim loved Riobaldo and longed to become his wife some day, but at first her role as a jagunço, supposedly imposed by her father, who used to say, she declares, that she needed to be "diferente, muito diferente" (105), and later her determination to avenge his murder, made her hide her identity from him. Yet, in spite of her male clothes and the respect she inspired in the other jagunços as a result of her bravery – which once led Riobaldo himself to say that she was "o único homem que a coragem dele nunca piscava; e que, por isso, foi o único cuja toda coragem às vezes eu invejei" (404) – she often behaved as a woman, particularly in the expression of her feelings, and transmitted to her friend, willingly or unwillingly, the tenderness of her affection.

This double role of Diadorim and her oscillating behavior endows the protagonist's conflict in the novel with a new dimension by revealing that its basic opposition, far from being one between a licit and an illicit kind of love, or between accepting and rejecting something considered illicit, is rather one between being an appearance, or, in other words, between one's capacity on the one hand or incapacity on the other to see beyond the apparent. For if Riobaldo's love for Diadorim was seen, as it was by Riobaldo at first, as sinful or illicit because of its homosexual appearance, the fact, discovered at the end, that it was inspired by a woman who in addition nourished it not only contradicts that former idea and reveals its other side as a licit and ordinary attraction, but also indicates the waste and uselessness of his suffering, caused by his incapacity to distinguish appearance from essence. A consciousness of this opposition and of its importance within the structure of the novel led Proença to state in *Trilhas no Grande sertão* that "a paixão do jagunço Riobaldo pelo moço Diadorim, não se parece, no seu primitivismo, com o refinamento de romancistas europeus lavrando no lusco-fusco de homossexualismo. Antes, nos recorda processo muito ao gosto do povo – o de dar aparência de imoralidade a fatos comuns – explorado, principalmente nas adivinhas como a da agulha, do macarrão, dos olhos, ou de João e Maria" (26).

Although the validity of the above statement may be contested by some critics who insist on discussing the licit or illicit character of Riobaldo's love, based on arguments such as the one that he did not know Diadorim's true sex and yet could not help loving her – let us add here that those who say so fail to see the role played by intuition in this case – the importance of the opposition between being and appearance is made evident at the end of the novel when, after the revelation of Diadorim's identity, Riobaldo's conflict with regard to their relationship disappears to give way to a feeling of guilt, caused by his incapacity to discover it earlier. This guilty feeling will remain throughout his life, and he will transmit it to his interlocutor when telling his story. By this time, aware of the secret of Diadorim, Riobaldo recollects all those elements which in the past clearly indicated her female identity, and blames himself for having been a victim of inadequate perception. Thus he asks: "Como foi que não tive um pressentimento?" (182).

This question, repeated several times throughout the narrative though in different forms, is a key element for the understanding of the novel, because it brings up the very issue of perception and expresses the theme of the relativity of things, present in almost every aspect of the structure of the work. In the same way that Riobaldo wondered, the reader may also ask how, having spent a long time in daily contact with Diadorim, he did not notice anything which might have indicated her sexual indentity. And, in fact, if one thinks about the physical traits of Diadorim, as described by Riobaldo, and about the great number of times when she behaves as a woman, the idea that he did not discover her true sex may appear as absurd, giving way to a magical interpretation that would infringe the laws of verisimilitude.

This interpretation, however, which would be perfectly acceptable within the sphere of allegory or symbolism, and also be plausible in the context of "magical realism," cannot be applicable to a novel like *Grande sertão: veredas,* in which the author never goes totally beyond the barriers of rationalistic perception. The evidence of this is the fact that the answer to such a question is present in the narrative itself, especially in two of its elements: the series of statements, often repeated with slight variations, that stress the relativity of perception in the apprehension of reality, and the structural device employed by the narrator of involving his interlocutor in his own process of narration.

Although the statements just mentioned are abundant in the novel and very significant to justify Riobaldo's failure of perception, they vary so little from one another that we will simply cite the following, in which he confesses: "Eu atravesso as coisas – e no meio da travessia não vejo! – só estva era entretido na idéia dos lugares de saída e de chegada" (35). Here, by using the image of the "travessia," so prominent in the entire narrative, Riobaldo makes it clear, as he confirms in a further passage, that he was too close to Diadorim and too emotionally involved to be able to see anything clearly: "Ele estava sempre tão perto demais de mim, e eu gostava demais dele" (357). And the reader, if not totally convinced, at least receives a plausible explanation for his not even having been able to grasp the meaning of the now-so-obvious words, pronounced by Diadorim, first at the moment of their entrance into the Liso de Sussuarão, and again on the day before the final battle:

—Riobaldo, o cumprir de nossa vingança vem perto... Daí, quando tudo estiver repag e refeito, um segredo, uma coisa, vou contar a você. (480)

and:

—Riobaldo, hoje-em-dia eu nem sei o que sei, e, o que soubesse, deixei de saber o que sabia.... Por vingar a morte de Joca Ramiro, vou, e vou e faço, consoante devo. Só, e Deus que me passe por esta, que indo vou não com meu coração que bate agora presente, mas com o coração de tempo passado... E digo...... Menos vou, também, punindo por meu pai Joca Ramiro, que é meu dever, do que por rumo de servir você, Riobaldo, no querer e cumprir. (502)

But if the first element may not be enough to justify, in terms of the narrative structure, Riobaldo's incapacity to discern appearance from essece, the issue seems to become clear when we think of the technique he employs of involving his interlocutor into his own process of narration, by extending to him the problem of perceiving or not the identity of Diadorim. Although the narrative of Riobaldo does not respect the chronological order of the facts narrated, he reveals to his interlocutor the secret of his friend only at the very moment in which he himself discovered it, and justifies his attitude by saying: "Eu conheci! Como em todo o tempo antes eu não contei ao senhor – e mercê peço – mas para o senhor divulgar comigo, a par, justo o travo de tanto segredo, sabendo somente no átimo em que eu também só soube.... Que Diadorim era o corpo de uma mulher, moça perfeita" (563). However, this device, which might seem at first glance merely a way of maintaining the narrative in suspense for the sake of keeping his interlocutor's interest, has here another function, namely that of testing the latter's perception and consequently of expressing, by that means, the theme of the relativity of things. Riobaldo wants his interlocutor to experience, through his narration, a process similar to that through which he has gone in his life, so that he may check whether the latter will or will not be able to find out, before he tells him, that which he himself could not discover. Thus he offers him, throughout the entire narrative, a series of hints ranging from the description of Diadorim's physical traits to the report of attitudes which, seen in retrospect, clearly indicate her true identity, and he comes to the point of almost telling everything:

> Diadorim era mais do ódio do que do amor? Me lembro, lembro dele nessa hora, nesse dia, tão remarcado. Como foi que não tive um pressentimento? O senhor mesmo, o senhor pode imaginar de ver um corpo claro e virgem de moça, morto à mão, esfaqueado, tinto todo de seu sangue, e os lábios da boca descorados no branquiço, os olhos dum terminado estilo, meio abertos meio fechados? E essa moça de quem o senhor gostou, que era um destino e uma surda esperança em sua vida?! Ah, Diadorim... E tantos anos já se passaram. (182)

But, since even in this case a certain ambiguity is maintained, whether the secret is discovered or not will depend entirely on the interlocutor's perception, and by extension the reader's, and will therefore vary from one person to another.

3.3. The Issue of Chance in Riobaldo's Life

Having seen how the ambiguous friendship Riobaldo devoted to Diadorim contributes to the neutralization of the opposition between objective realism and other levels of reality in the novel, we will now briefly discuss the other element mentioned which also strongly contributes to such a neutralization, namely the role played by chance in the course of the protagonist's life.

We have seen, when discussing Riobaldo's status as a jagunço, that although he very much admired the latter's way of life he could not accept the idea of becoming a jagunço himself and tried as hard as he could to avoid entering a group. Yet he eventually leads the life of a jagunço, first on Zé Bebelo's side and finally on Joca Ramiro's side. In both these cases, however, Riobaldo was driven to the groups as a result of chance, and the events that led him to take such a step occurred precisely in moments in which he was attempting to give his life a different direction: in the first case, he had accepted a job as a private instructor to a man whom he did not know was fighting the jagunços, and in the second he was fleeing from Zé Bebelo's group when, by means of a woman with whom he had spent the night, he ran into Diadorim and was impelled to remain on his side.

In the same way that Riobaldo was driven more than once to become a jagunço in spite of all his efforts to escape the role, each time he thinks about abandoning this life during his marches through the backlands something happens which makes him change his mind. The result is that, far from setting himself apart from the jagunços' world, he gets constantly more involved with it, and finally becomes not only his group's leader but also the very man who restores the equilibrium of that world. The events which prevented Riobaldo from leaving the jagunços' world were listed by Proença in *Trilhas no Grande sertão*, together with others which, also fortuitous, had a significant effect upon his life. The following could be mentioned as examples: the capture of Zé Bebelo, which caused his trial and, as a consequence, the murder of Joca Ramiro; Zé Bebelo's errors as a leader, which led Riobaldo to contract the pact with the devil and assume the command of the troops; his failure to meet Nhorinhá for the second time and the eight-year delay of her letter to him, which prevented him from marrying her and settling down peacefully in a backlands retreat; and finally his absence at the time the final battle began, which led him to alter his carefully elaborated plans and made way for the confrontation of Hermógenes and Diadorim that resulted in their killing each other.

These events, all marked by the presence of an element that can be characterized by its function of altering that which was being planned or expected by the protagonist, indicate the existence of a theme in the narrative of *Grande sertão: veredas* which contains a clear allusion to the myth of Oedipus the King – that of a man who, no matter how much he may try, cannot escape from his destiny – and consequently reveal the presence of a world view based on a mythical-sacred order. Like Oedipus, Riobaldo has spent a great part of his life trying to escape from things which he could not accept, to the point of becoming, as he himself declares, a "fugidor," who has run away "até da precisão de fuga" (176), and later in his life he realizes, in the same way as the Greek king, that all his attempts were useless and that he was nothing more than "um pobre menino do destino" (18), whose mission was "dar cabo definitivo do Hermógenes, naquele dia, naquele lugar" (540). Now that Riobaldo has gone through his experience as a jagunço and has suffered a great deal as a result of it, he seems to have come to the conclusion that there was some kind of predestination for his life, and affirms to his interlocutor: "Existe uma receita, a norma dum caminho certo, estreito, de cada uma pessoa viver – e essa pauta cada um tem – mas a gente mesmo, no comum, não sabe encontrar" (456).

However, in spite of the existence in the novel of the theme mentioned above and of the obvious parallel with the story of Oedipus the King, the treatment given the issue of destiny in *Grande sertão: veredas* does not presuppose the existence of any supernatural being and therefore, like the other elements we have discussed, does not exclude the possibility of a rational explanation for it. In contrast to what happens in the Greek world, where man's destiny is often predicted by an oracle and the influence of the gods is constantly made evident, destiny in Rosa's novel is not presented by the narrator as having, as Benedito Nunes puts it, "a eficácia de uma força exterior e independente" ("Guimarães Rosa," p. 178). And although Riobaldo's actions follow, as the critic observes, "a linha itinerante de caminhos que se apartam e se entrecruzam, para se unirem depois, produzindo pela convergência de causas mínimas, imprevisiveis, circunstanciais, um efeito único, que parece pré-ordenado por uma *razão*... exterior aos atos humanos" (ibid., p. 175), the *razão* referred to here is never presented as a divine imposition, but rather simply as something unexplainable which, for this very reason, is found strange by the protagonist.

But while the fact that there does not exist in *Grande sertão: veredas* any supernatural being who would predict the course of one's life or interfere in one's actions may not eliminate the possibility of existence in the narrative of a logical-rational world view, neither does it indicate a subordination of the mythical world view mentioned above to any sort of rationalistic conception. In the same way that the magical character of destiny is never made evident in the novel, there is no moment in it in which destiny is presented in rationalistic terms as a mere product of cause and effect. Throughout the entire report that Riobaldo presents to his interlocutor he limits himself to narrating those events that seem strange to him, and expresses a desire to know the factors which have determined these events by raising a series of questions such as:

> Se eu não tivesse passado por um lugar, uma mulher, a combinação daquela mulher acender a fogueira, eu nunca mais, nesta vida, tinha topado com o Menino? (136)

or

> Em sua vida é assim? Na minha, agora é que vejo, as coisas importantes, todas, em caso curto de acaso foi que se conseguiram – pelo pulo fino de sem ver se dar – a sorte momenteira, por cabelo por um fio, um clim de clina de cavalo. Ah, e se não fosse, cada acaso, não tivesse sido, qual é então que teria sido o meu destino seguinte? (120-21)

But, since at no moment whatsoever does he provide any answer to the questions posed, all sorts of explanations, be they of a mythical or of a rational character, are made possible and become equally valid in the realm of the novel.

The questions above, as well as several others of the same sort raised throughout the narrative, indicate a suspicion on the part of the narrator that there is some kind of predestination determining the events of his life. But since no answer is given to any of the questions, yielding indiscriminately to a mythical or a rational explanation for the nature of such a predestination, the issue is left open, revealing once again the oscillation of the protagonist between two worlds of a different order. If on the one hand Riobaldo is inclined to accept the supernatural character of destiny and thereby justify all his past actions, he is on the other hand dissatisfied with such an attitude, and consequently questions the exclusive character of both the views we have presented. Thus if destiny is present in *Grande sertão: veredas* it is not seen, at least from the point of view of Riobaldo, either exclusively as a fatalistic force in the Greek or even in the Christian sense of the term, or simply as a product of a series of facts based on a sequence of cause and effect, but rather only as something indefinable which embraces as possibilities all these different traditional views. In this sense the issue of destiny, as presented in the novel, plays a decisive role for the neutralization of the opposition we have been discussing, and confirms the idea that the world view represented here is based on a total or all-encompassing notion of realism.

4. *Grande Sertão: Veredas*: A Committed Novel

> Revolucionar a língua é a mais profunda revolução que se pode fazer; sem ela, a revolução das idéias é apenas aparente.
>
> Miguel de Unamuno

> A Revolução é, antes de tudo, um ato de poesia.
>
> Franklin de Oliveira

4.1. *The Revitalization of Language*

The neutralization of the third and last opposition with which we are concerned here – that between aestheticism and social commitment – constitutes a fundamental aspect of our conception of *Grande sertão: veredas* as a synthesis novel, not only because it is directly associated with the neutralization of the two other oppositions we have discussed previously, but also because it confers upon the book a status which distinguishes it from several other contemporary novels that, while also having expressed a strong preoccupation with form, can be considered pure verbal experiments and have been accused by critics of alienation. This neutralization and its consequences for *Grande sertão: veredas* will be the object of discussion in this part of our study.

When *Grande sertão: veredas* was published, in 1956, critics were so impressed with the number of linguistic and structural innovations which it presented that they dedicated a series of studies, some of a very high quality, to this aspect of the work, neglecting somewhat other aspects which generally had been given more attention in the works of earlier novelists – namely those aspects traditionally included under the general label of "content." Although practically irrelevant now, this fact had a significant importance in the years immediately following publication of the novel, because it led to the criticism that Rosa's preoccupation with form was so strong that he had subordinated everything in his novel to it and disregarded the social or historical context which had served as a point of departure.

There is no doubt that the aestheticist preoccupation in *Grande sertão: veredas* was extremely relevant, to the point of partially justifying the criticism it has received, but the second part of the above argument – that Guimarães Rosa had disregarded the social or historical context on which the novel was based – is unfounded and was more recently contested by critics who studied the work from a sociological perspective. As much as any so-called socially committed novel, *Grande sertão: veredas* offers a critical view of Brazilian rural society at a certain time of its history – namely the period which has become known as that of the "Old Republic" (1889-1930) – and it constitutes, as Nogueira Galvão has said, "o mais profundo e completo estudo até hoje feito sobre a plebe rural brasileira" (Galvão, p. 74). But it is distinguished from that type of novel by the fact that the criticism of society present there, rather than being explicit, is accomplished through language and the experience of the characters; in other words, through the literary elements which compose the work. And since Brazilians were accustomed to a kind of novel whose main purpose was to criticize society explicitly, they failed to see this aspect of Rosa's book and developed a negative reaction to it.

But the great mistake into which those who see *Grande sertão: veredas* as an apolitical or alienated work have fallen does not derive merely from their familiarity with a different kind of novel but also, and most especially, from an old prejudice, which found fertile ground in Latin America in the first half of the twentieth century, according to which the form and the content of a narrative art work were two independent elements and the former was important only as a vehicle for the transmission of the latter. Influenced by this monocular view of the novel and imbued with the idea that the function of literature was to denounce the negative aspects of society for the purpose of causing a change in the present state of things, these people failed to see that Rosa's preoccupation with form, far from being a pure aestheticist obsession, as they have inferred, is rather a conscious political attitude, based on an entire revolutionary program; they did not recognize the value of a novel which, even from the sociopolitical point of view, is one of the most revolutionary in twentieth-century Brazilian literature.

Contrary to the mentality still dominant when *Grande sertão: veredas* was published, Guimarães Rosa believed, as he declares in his interview with Günter Lorenz, that in the same way that the sound and the meaning of a word depend on each other, the form and the content of a literary work cannot be dissociated. He criticizes those writers who, because of excessive preoccupation with the ideas they want to express, do not recognize the importance of language in a literary composition: "Estos jóvenes que declaran abiertamente que ya no se trata más del idioma, que sólo el contenido tiene valor, son pobres estudiantes dignos de lástima" (Lorenz, "Diálogo," p. 42). These young men to whom he refers believed they were producing a revolutionary kind of art because they denounced the oppressive social reality of their countries, but since they accomplished their task by means of a traditional type of language, their works can hardly be said to be truly revolutionary, for, as he states, "el mejor de los contenidos no vale nada si el idioma no le hace justicia" (ibid.).

Since Guimarães Rose was aware of the dialectical relationship which exists between the aesthetic object and the outside world, he felt as much as the above writers the necessity of offering his readers a new world view that might cause them to question their own system of values, but unlike those writers he believed that "solamente renovando el idioma se puede renovar el mundo" (ibid.). For Rosa, the language of a people is intimately connected with this people's way of thinking, with its own view of the world. Thus, if one wishes to alter this world view, it is necessary to start by changing the language which reflects it; only in this way could an author free this people from its old categories of thought. It is not possible, Guimarães Rosa thinks, to offer a people a new world view by means of a type of language that is linked to a former reality, for the resulting gap between the author's conscience and his language would make his effort unfruitful. The revolution in the novel has to start from within, from the literary form itself, and with this in mind Rosa sets himself the task of revolutionizing the language and structure of narrative.

As we have seen in the first section of this study, the type of language employed by most Latin American writers of the 20's and 30's was associated with a one-sided and obsolete world view — that of the realist and naturalist writers of the late nineteenth century — and as such it was unfit to represent the reality of twentieth-century man. It was, as we have stated, "a descriptive kind of language, crystallized in stereotyped formulas, which did not go beyond appearance and the conventional" (see p. 32 above). This frozen type of language was appropriate to represent a static world, measurable by rational categories, but when used to express a different world view it is insufficient, and a gap is immediately established between the world presented and the way of presenting it. Conscious of the existence of such a gap in the works of the committed Latin American authors of the twentieth century and of the impossibility of expressing his world view by means of this sort of language, Guimarães Rosa decided to break with the conventionality of this language and to search for a more flexible expression that might possibly transmit the conception of reality of the man of his time. His breaking of the conventionality of such a language and his consequent search for a new expression, free from labels or clichés, constitutes Guimarães Rosa's revolution of the language and structure of narrative.

This aesthetic revolution which Guimarães Rosa undertook in his works does not imply, however, as it was believed for some time, a total rupture with Brazilian literary tradition, nor does it by any means indicate the creation of a new language, dissociated from his own. It is true that Guimarães Rosa seriously infringed the norm of the Portuguese language and was as a result somewhat hermetic in his works, but at no time did he disregard the system of this language nor did he ever attempt to cross the barriers it imposed.[16] Rather, what he did was to explore the various potentialities within this very system and restore the poetic character of that type of language, effaced in the works of his predecessors. This is what Proença, who studied the issue in detail, concluded in *Trilhas no Grande sertão:*

> Ainda que se considerem língua e dialeto com o máximo de amplitude semântica, ainda assim não houve criação. O que ocorreu foi ampla utilização de virtualidades da nossa língua, tendo a analogia, principalmente, fornecido os recursos de que ele se serviu para construir uma fala capaz de refletir a enorme carga afetiva do seu discurso. Daí, embora reconhecendo que, pela abundante contribuição individual, essa fala encontra dificuldades para se incorporar à *língua*, não cabe falar em criação, mas em esforço consciente no sentido de uma evolução da linguagem literária. (Pp. 75-76)

This exploration of the potentialities present within the system of his own language and his resultant restoration of the poetic character of the language are precisely what has been called by critics Rosa's revitalization of the literary language. The poetic character of a language, which consists exactly of its capacity to suggest more than what is basically meant by the words selected in a discourse and by their combination into phrases and sentences, is weakened or diluted every time the signs of this language are employed to express fixed or conventional concepts. When this phenomenon occurs, words lose the variety of their potential meanings, expressions are deprived of their original energy, and syntax abandons its infinite possibilities and has its scope reduced to ready-made sentences and stereotypes; in other words, language undergoes a process of exhaustion and becomes incapable of expressing new concepts and ideas. It is necessary, then, to revitalize the language, to make it recover its original strength; to do so the writer has to violate the norm of the language and substitute for the commonplace the unique, abandon worn-out form and search for the unexplored – the new metal which lay

---

[16] For the linguistic concepts of "system" and "norm" see Eugenio Coseriu, *Sistema, norma y habla* (Montevideo: Universidad de la República, 1952).

hidden, as Rosa himself says, "bajo montañas de cenizas" (Lorenz, "Diálogo," p. 39).

An interesting example of this process of revitalization on the level of language stricto sensu is given by Rosa in an interview with Fernando Camacho, in which he explains his use of a neologism in a story from *Primeiras estórias:*

> Quando eu digo "circuntristeza" não é para fazer uma palavra nova, é porque tenho que dizer que tudo estava triste, mas sem usar linhas que quebram a perspectiva, sem estruturas muito pesadas senão não voa. Tudo influi. O negócio é como na música, uma nota, só uma, uma pausa, uma vírgula é importante, conta.... Então, em vez de "circuntristeza," outro diria assim: "Ele estava tão triste, cheio de melancolia" ou que "ele vivia triste, que tudo lhe parecia triste, desde o horizonte, a paisagem, tudo." Agora quando eu digo "na circuntristeza" está dito o almanaque todinho, com toda sua força mas sem gastar espaço.[17]

The phrases mentioned in the passage are denotatively equivalent to the construction created by Rosa, but they do not have the poetic connotation of the expression *na circuntristeza*. They are a referential kind of language, worn out by usage, which fails to transmit the intensity of the emotion the writer wishes to express. To transmit this emotion, therefore, the author abandons these constructions and replaces them with an expression, never before employed, which contains a wide spectrum of semantic possibilities. He thereby certainly infringes the norm of the Portuguese language, but the new construction, far from constituting a rupture with the system of this language, is rather the result of his exploitation of the potentialities of this system: the prefix *circum*, of Latin origin, though never before used with the noun *tristeza*, is frequently employed, with the same meaning, before other nouns in Portuguese (e.g., *circunavegação, circunlocução, circunvizinhança*).

This process of revitalization which Rosa accomplished is not limited, as one might suppose, to the various aspects of language understood in the strict sense of a physical, acoustic entity and its

---

[17] Fernando Camacho, "Entrevista com João Guimarães Rosa," *Humboldt*, No. 37 (1978), p. 48.

written counterpart; for the term "language," as we have seen, also includes the form of a literary piece, the syntax, lexicon, and morphology of a narrative work of art. And in the same way that the language stricto sensu of a narrative undergoes a process of exhaustion, the form of such a work also ages and becomes inexpressive after some time. It is necessary, then, to revitalize it, to make it regain its original expressiveness, and to achieve this goal the writer must employ tools similar to those he has used in relation to the aspects of his language: he has to cause a rupture in the norm and explore the potentialities of the genre form he has selected.

Since the procedures employed by Guimarães Rosa to break with the norm of the Portuguese language and explore the potentialities latent within its system were varied and numerous, and have been studied exhaustively by several critics,[18] we will not review them here. We will concentrate on the procedures used on the level of narrative discourse – that is, the innovations the author introduced into the narrative structure of his works, and specifically into the framework of *Grande sertão: veredas*. We will not focus on each of these procedures separately, nor discuss in detail the role each of them has had in breaking with the traditional form of the genre; such an enumeration, however important, is beyond the scope of this study. Rather, we will present a general view of these intimately connected procedures, in an attempt to discover how they serve the author's purpose, which was to offer the reader a new world view that might lead him to question his own system of values, creating thereby a process of searching equivalent to the one that he himself experienced.

4.2. *The Search for Expression: Living vs. Narrating*

Seen from this perspective, one of the most significant structural innovations which Guimarães Rosa introduced into the

---

[18] Some of these studies are: Cavalcânti Proença, *Trilhas no Grande sertão;* Oswaldino Marques, "Canto e plumagem das palavras," in *Ensaios escolhidos;* Mary Daniel, *João Guimarães Rosa: travessia literária;* and Eduardo F. Coutinho, *The Process of Revitalization of the Language and Narrative Structure in the Fiction of João Guimarães Rosa and Julio Cortázar.* For complete bibliographical references, see section III of Bibliography.

narrative discourse of his *Grande sertão: veredas* is, in our view, that the entire novel is constructed in the form of a question. Riobaldo is tormented with the idea that he had sold his soul to the devil, but he is not entirely sure the devil actually exists; thus he decides to narrate his life to an interlocutor in order to pose this question to him at the end. This purpose of the narrative is made explicit several times in the novel, as for example when Riobaldo says: "De tudo não falo. Não tenciono relatar ao senhor minha vida em dobrados passos; servia para que? Quero é armar o ponto dum fato, para depois lhe pedir um conselho. Por daí, então careço de que o senhor escute bem essas passagens: da vida de Riobaldo, o jagunço" (205-06), or when he states: "Conto ao senhor é o que eu sei e o senhor não sabe; mas principal quero contar é o que eu não sei se sei, e que pode ser que o senhor saiba" (217). Riobaldo feels guilty for having contracted a pact with the devil and blames himself for the death of his friend Diadorim, which he considers a consequence of that, and sets himself the task of reporting the events of his life which preceded and followed that pact in the hope of finding some relief for his conscience, some kind of judgment or even pardon. Everything in his narrative converges toward the final question which, not finding any convincing answer, is left open for the reader to reflect upon.

If Riobaldo's narrative is all directed toward a central question, as he declared, such a narrative is also in and of itself a question in the sense that it is constructed in a sort of language defined precisely by its searching character, by its speculative aspect. Riobaldo is a representation of man in a state of doubt, of uncertainty, who wants to "decifrar as coisas que são importantes" (96); thus his narrative, instead of being a mere report of past facts or events, is a speculation about those facts, a constant attempt to interpret or find a meaning for them. His speculations are never definitive, because the answers he comes up with carry in themselves a series of new questions, bringing him into a dialectical process which could terminate only at the time of his own death; for this reason, his entire narrative is, more than anything else, a posing of problems, which he invites his interlocutor to discuss. To see how this posing of problems operates in *Grande sertão: veredas*, originating a kind of narrative that inquires more than it affirms, we will show how its various levels are combined to produce this effect.

At the beginning of the long narrative about his former life as a jagunço and the consequences of that experience, Riobaldo, by this time an aged farmer, says: "De primeiro, eu fazia e mexia, e pensar não pensava. Não possuía os prazos. Vivi puxando difícil de difícel, peixe vivo no moquém: quem mói no asp'ro, não fantaseia. Mas, agora, feita a folga que me vem, e sem pequenos dessossegos, estou de range-rede. E me inventei neste gosto, de especular idéia" (11). In this passage, which constitutes a kind of summary of the structure of *Grande sertão: veredas*, the reader can clearly see that the narrative which Riobaldo has just begun to recount is constructed around two basic lines, or levels, associated with two different moments of his life and marked by two different attitudes on his part—namely, a past time during which he experienced the facts he is narrating now, predominantly marked by his action in the sertão; and a present time, characterized by a speculative attitude, in which he is reporting those past events to his interlocutor and is experiencing them again in the very act of narration. Although these two lines cannot be separated—they are interwoven on every level of the narrative and its total effect comes precisely from their integration, a synthesis of apparently opposing terms—we will here focus on each of them at a time and show how they are combined in the corpus of the novel.

The first of these lines, the past, corresponds to the story which Riobaldo set out to tell—that is, the story of his life as a jagunço, and it is composed of those episodes which occurred at that time. However, since these episodes are of two entirely distinct kinds, we can easily distinguish here the presence of two sublines: an objective one, formed by the succession of external facts and events with which the narrator-protagonist is involved in the backlands, i.e., his battles and toils, and a subjective one, constituted by the inner conflicts he had at that time, e.g., his hesitation between the love of Otacília and that of Nhorinhá, his simultaneous attraction and repulsion for Diadorim and his fear of assuming the command of his troops. These two sublines, different though they may be because of the nature of their component episodes and conflicts and of the aim pursued by the protagonist in each of them (in the former that which is sought is the equilibrium of the jagunço's world, and in the latter Riobaldo's personal happiness), are nevertheless very similar in their structure, and their movement, alternating throughout the entire narrative, is revealed as convergent at the end, when they merge into a single climax – a final battle which results in the death of Diadorim and the revelation of his/her true sex.

The second of these lines – the time of narration – is composed of the experiences which the narrator-protagonist is going through at the very moment in which he is reporting his past life to his interlocutor – that is, his speculations about those facts or events and his attempt to organize them into narrative terms. Here again we can clearly distinguish the presence of two sublines, one basically speculative and the other critical and metalinguistic. In the former the narrator is preoccupied with deciphering those things he could not understand until then, and dissipating the doubts which continue to torment him; in the latter he is concerned with his own way of narrating those things, with finding the most suitable expression to transmit them with a maximum of faithfulness. These two sublines differ fundamentally from those of the past in that they exist only in the act of narration – they are exclusively a verbal experience, but they also differ from one another in that in the first case language is an object per se, that is, it is itself a means and an end; in the second it is the object of another language, that is, a metalanguage.[19]

But if these two lines around which the narrative is constructed can be clearly distinguished because they correspond to two different moments in the life of the narrator-protagonist and two different attitudes on his part – in the first case he experiences that which he will later narrate and in the second he narrates that which he has formerly experienced – they are mutually dependent in the novel, for if the narrator's present speculations are a consequence of his actions in the past, the latter are important only insofar as they are still alive within the present, in the form of questions which torment him now. Riobaldo's narrative is neither a mere report of past facts and events nor a simple accumulation of a number of present speculations, but rather a fusion of these two modalities or genres; and precisely in this fusion lies its basic tension: a will on the part of the narrator to reconstruct with some

---

[19] For further elucidation of this point, see my *The Process of Revitalization of the Language and Narrative Structure*... (Valencia: Albatros Ediciones – Hispanófila, 1980), pp. 68-69, in which I discuss the use of metalinguistics as a process of narrative technique.

exactness the events of his past life to dissipate his present doubts and anxieties, and a consciousness of the impossibility of doing so, at least in the terms desired, owing to the time gap between one moment and the other and the difficulty of molding living experiences into the medium of language.

This tension can be clearly evidenced if we contrast, for example, the order of Riobaldo's narrative with his constant preoccupation about the chronology of the past events. *Grande sertão: veredas* begins in the present, the time of narration, with the episode of the calf already mentioned, and ends in the present, at the moment in which Riobaldo, having finished his story to his interlocutor, puts to him the question which motivated the entire narration. Yet, throughout its development the facts and events of the past alternate with the narrator's present speculations and are basically ordered according to the way they come afloat in his memory. And since in one's memory the episodes of the past are almost never registered in the order in which they actually occurred, the result is a predominantly achronological discourse, provoking in the reader an impression of chaos that is totally dissipated only at the end, when he sees the narrative as a whole.

However, while Riobaldo constructs his narrative in this somewhat chaotic order, responsible for its to and fro movement so much discussed by critics, he also reveals a strong preoccupation about the chronology of his past life and often interrupts his report to make comments such as: "Ai, arre, mas: que esta minha boca não tem ordem nenhuma. Estou contando fora, coisas divagadas" (21), or "Sei que estou contando errado, pelos altos. Desemendo. Mas não é por disfarçar, não pense. De grave, na lei do comum, disse ao senhor quase tudo. Não crio receio" (94). And every time he feels that the reader may become too confused because of the order in which he has arranged his material, he provides an explanation that sets every element in its proper place:

> Essas coisas todas se passaram tempos depois. Talhei de avanço em minha história. O senhor tolere minhas más devassas no contar. É ignorância. Eu não converso com ninguém de fora, quase. Não sei contar direito.... Agora ... é que aos poucos vou indo aprendendo a contar corrigido. E para o dito volto. (189)

or

> E foi assim que a gente principiou a tristonha história de tantas caminhadas e vagos combates, e sofrimentos, que já relatei ao senhor, se não me engano até ao ponto em que Zé Bebelo voltou, com cinco homens, descendo o rio Paracatu numa balsa de talos de buriti; e herdou brioso comando; e o que debaixo de Zé Bebelo fomos fazendo, bimbando vitórias, acho que eu disse até um fogo que demos, bem dado e bem ganho, na Fazenda São Serafim. Mas isso, o senhor então já sabe. (292)

Since the narrator is conscious of the fact that he is reporting the episodes of his life in a predominantly achronological-manner, he uses such devices to help his interlocutor locate them in time; but he is also conscious that he could not adopt a different procedure in his narrative and justifies his position by saying: "Eu estou contando assim, porque é o meu jeito de contar. Guerras e batalhas? Isso é como jogo de baralho, verte, reverte" (95); and later:

> A lembrança da vida da gente se guarda em trechos diversos, cada um com seu signo eseu sentimento, uns com os outros acho que nem não misturam. Contar seguido, alinhavado, só mesmo sendo as coisas de rasa importância. De cada vivimento que eu real tive, de alegria forte ou pesar, cada vez daquela hoje vejo que eu era como se fosse diferente pessoa. Sucedido desgovernado. Assim eu acho, assim é que eu conto. O senhor é bondoso de me ouvir. Tem horas antigas que ficaram muito mais perto da gente do que outras, de recente data. O senhor mesmo sabe. (95)

If, as Riobaldo says, there are moments in his past life which are closer to him than others of a more recent date, there is no point in narrating those moments in a chronological order. The episodes of his past that have been stored in his memory emerge in the present according to the importance they had and still have for him now, which is usually determined by the intensity of the experience; thus they must be reported in the order they occur in his mind. But at this point the narrator is faced with a problem: since this is a subjective criterion of importance, he is always suspicious that he might be distorting things, and he expresses such a feeling in passages like the following:

> Ah, mas falo falso. O senhor sente? Desmente? Eu desminto. Contar é muito, muito dificultoso. Não pelos anos que se já passaram. Mas pela astúcia que têm certas coisas passadas – de fazer balancê, de se remexerem dos lugares. O que eu falei foi exato? Foi. Mas teria sido? Agora, acho que nem não. São tantas horas de pessoas, tantas coisas em tantos tempos, tudo miúdo recruzado. (175)

This issue of the chronology constitutes a fundamental element in the novel in the sense that it expresses, better perhaps than any other, the tension which takes hold of the narrator-protagonist at the time he sets out to report his life to his interlocutor. Yet, since from a general perspective this issue is merely a part, albeit representative, of a more complex whole – the problem of reconstructing the past – we will examine the latter now. And we will begin by recalling the two reasons given for the impossibility of accomplishing this reconstruction with a maximum of faithfulness: the time span between the occurrence of the episodes Riobaldo is reporting and their reconstitution in his narrative, and the difficulty of molding living experiences into the medium of language. But before we go any further into the subject matter, let us mention that whereas the first reason is directly associated with time – that is, with the narrator's consciousness of the dynamic character of reality – the second is basically a question of what we could call here "space" – the adaptation of a certain reality into another which, though of a different sort, is there to represent the former.[20]

The first of these reasons – the question of the time span – can be clearly seen if we think of two elements which constitute a constant preoccupation for Riobaldo – namely his consciousness of

---

[20] The reality of language (as well as that of the work of art) is a reality of its own, independent from that of the outside world; thus, whenever one wishes to represent a living experience through language (whether by simply narrating it or through the creation of a work of art), this person will always have to face the problem of molding or adapting a certain reality into another of a different sort, that is, of molding or adapting the reality of the outside world into that of language.

the selective character of memory, and of the impossibility of separating past from present, or the events of one's past life from the view one has of them in the present. As far as the first element is concerned, it suffices to recall the following passage, in which the narrator declares: "O senhor entende, o que conto assim é resumo; pois, no estado do viver, as coisas vão enqueridas com muita astúcia: um dia é todo para a esperança, o seguinte para a desconsolação" (387). As we can see, Riobaldo knows very well that what he is narrating is not his entire life as a jagunço but simply a summary of that life, or: "as coisas que formaram passado para mim com mais pertença" (99), for the others have been blurred in his mind and lost in the mazes of time. Here another problem, similar to the chronology one, can be pointed out: the criterion of selection utilized by one's memory is subjective, and the narrator, aware of this fact, raises the question of whether he might not be offering his interlocutor a tendentious view of his past. He knows that he could not have acted otherwise because of the very nature of reality, which cannot be approached from a static perspective, but the mere consciousness of this fact does not help to eliminate his conflict. Hence his need to explain the reasons for his narrating something: "E o senhor me desculpe, de estar retrasando em tantas minudências. Mas até hoje eu represento em meus olhos aquela hora, tudo tão bom; e, o que é, é saudade" (114); or to support his inclusion of a certain episode in the narrative with the opinion of other people:

> As partes, que se deram ou não se deram, ali na Barbaranha, eu aplico, não por vezo meu de dar delongas e empalhar o tempo maior do senhor como meu ouvinte. Mas só porque o compadre meu Quelemém deduziu que os fatos daquela era faziam significado de muita importância em minha vida verdadeira, e entradamente o caso relatado pelo seo Ornelas, que com a lição solerte do Dr. Hilário se tinha formado. Aí, narro. O senhor me releve e suponha. (434)

The other element we have mentioned as an example of the time span problem – the narrator's consciousness of the fact that he can no longer separate the events of his past life from his present speculations about them – is also expressed in passages such as the following, in which Riobaldo comments:

> O senhor sabe?: não acerto no contar, porque estou remexendo o vivido longe alto, com pouco caroço, querendo esquentar, demear, de feito, meu coração, naquelas lembranças. Ou quero enfiar a idéia, achar o rumorzinho forte das coisas, caminho do que houve e do que não houve. As vezes não é fácil. Fé que não é. (167-68)

The narrator knows very well, as we can detect, that he is approaching the events of his past from the point of view of the present, mixing them with a certain amount of interpretation, and he is conscious, as in the case of his memory, that he could not do otherwise because of the time that has elapsed between one moment and the other. However, again as in the former case, the mere consciousness of this fact does not eliminate the conflict, and he wonders up to what point he might not be distorting his past by submitting everything to his own personal vision. This suspicion about the interpretative character of his present view of things drives him to declare, as above, that he does not know how to narrate, or to insist that it is not at all easy to do so.

These conflicts are not, however, exclusively related to time elapsed between the occurrence of those episodes and their reconstruction in his narrative, but also – and here we have the second reason his past cannot be faithful reconstituted – to the difficulty of molding his experiences into the medium of language. If reality is so fluid and multifaceted that he cannot faithfully reconstruct past episodes in the present, how can he transmit those episodes to his interlocutor without distorting them even further by making use of a medium which constitutes a different reality? Riobaldo is aware of the fact that every form of narrative, no matter how close it may seem to the reality it is representing, is always something different – another reality which exists per se, an object created in language – so that every attempt at transmitting his experiences through language will necessarily imply some distortion. That is why he asks his interlocutor:

> Mas, como vou contar ao senhor? Ao que narro, assim refiro, e esvaziado, luiz-e-silva. O senhor não sabe, o senhor não vê. Conto o que fiz? O que adjaz.... Como vou contar, e o senhor sentir em meu estado? O senhor sobrenasceu lá? O senhor mordeu aquilo? O senhor conheceu Diadorim, meu senhor?!...

Ah, o senhor pensa que morte é choro e sofisma – terra funda e ossos quietos. (557)

Yet while the narrator is conscious that narrating inevitably implies some kind of distortion, he also knows that this is the only way he has for re-experiencing his past; thus the problem posed to him becomes one of degree. Rather than being worried about the distortion of the facts he is narrating, therefore, his preoccupation concerns the degree of such distortion, and he will look for a type of language which seems most appropriate to express those facts.

This search for a new type of language is not an isolated element, then, but rather a conscious attitude on Riobaldo's part to offer his interlocutor a narration with a minimum of distortion. The language of the Latin American narrative of the 20's and 30's has become associated with a static and one-sided view of the world, and since the reality Riobaldo wants to express is one which transcends such a view, he would never be able to attain his aim by using that type of language. Aware of this fact, he has set himself the task of looking for a new expression and has established an isomorphic relationship between his world view and the way of expressing it by building his report into a poetic sort of language that is being created at the very moment of narration. This isomorphic relationship between the world view the narrator wants to represent and the way to represent it is credited by some critics, among whom José Carlos Garbuglio, in great part for the success of the narrative. (Garbuglio, pp. 88-89).

However, the great success which the narrator of *Grande sertão: veredas* achieved in terms of the representation of reality is not exclusively related to the type of language used, but also and most especially to the identification he has established between his language and his world view, by representing the search which characterizes the latter through the quest for a new expression. Riobaldo is a man who, self-admittedly, knows little but who is suspicious of many things ("Eu quase que nada não sei. Mas desconfio de muita coisa" [16]) – a man in a constant state of uncertainty and search. He uses narration to acomplish his search – it is itself a process of search, but since this process can be effected only if he finds a new type of language that inquires more than it affirms, an identification occurs between living and narrating, and his existential quest is represented through the search for a new expression. Thus, in addition to representing his world view through a type of language which, by its inquisitive character, best suits such a function, the narrator does so by using a process similar to that which characterizes his view, and constructs his entire report under the sign of search.

At this point we are faced with a problem which requires further comment: if on the one hand the identification existing between language and reality accounts for attenuating the degree of distortion effected by the narrator while reporting his experiences, on the other the experimental status of this language increases his doubts regarding its capacity to represent his world view. As Nogueira Galvão said in *As formas do falso*, language as it is conceived in *Grande sertão: veredas* is always a twofold element, and as such it can also be "um meio de minar a certeza e criar novamente a incerteza" (p. 128). This element of ultimate doubt, present on every level of the narrative of *Grande sertão: veredas* is indicated by the leitmotifs so frequently repeated through the entire text in the parallel constructions "Viver é muito perigoso" and "Contar é muito, muito dificultoso." Living is very dangerous because, as Riobaldo explains, "Aprender-a-viver é que é o viver, mesmo" (550) – and narrating, in its turn, is an arduous task in the sense that it is a modus vivendi, a part of man's living process, a voyage to the unknown. The narrative of Riobaldo is not the mere report of facts and events dead or petrified in a remote past, but rather a part of his life, a phase in a process of growth that is constantly being questioned and reformulated – a dialectical process with no definite end. And since in a dialectical process a term cannot exist without its negative counterpart and what is seen as a thesis at a certain moment can be revealed as an antithesis at another, Riobaldo's narrative can, in fine, be said to consist of a single great inquiry, one which questions simultaneously the reality it is intended to represent and the means of representing it.

4.3. *The Monologue-Dialogue Technique*

Having seen how Riobaldo's narrative is conceived as a great inquiry, as a process *in fieri* which never reaches a terminal point – let us not forget the symbol of infinity which follows the last words of the narrator – we will proceed now to a brief comment on the technique employed in this narrative, which we can define, following Roberto Schwarz, as a dialogue-monologue, or in his own words, "diálogo pela metade, ou diálogo visto por uma face" or "monólogo *inserto* em situação dialógica."[21]

If we take a quick look at the way the narrative of *Grande sertão: veredas* is composed, we immediately recognize in it a dialogical situation in which a certain narrator – Riobaldo, an uncultivated man from the backlands – makes a report to an interlocutor about his former life as a jagunço, and the latter – a cultivated urban citizen – listens carefully to the entire story and takes a series of notes which will serve him later as the basis for a possible book. However, in spite of the presence of a specific interlocutor, which confers an oral status on the narrator's report, the dialogical character of the situation just described is questioned by the reader when he realizes that at no moment throughout the entire novel is Riobaldo's narration interrupted to give way to the interlocutor's speech. On the contrary, it consists of a single flux, a continuum, and the listener's presence is evidenced only by the narrator's own remarks: the insistent reiteration of the form *o senhor* (formal equivalent of the pronoun "you") with which he always addresses him; a series of direct allusions which describe him as a man of great knowledge and sensibility ("Inveja minha pura é de uns conforme o senhor, com toda leitura e suma doutoração" [15]; or "O que eu prezava ter era essa instrução do senhor, que dá rumo para se estudar dessas matérias" [221]); and the frequent use of narrative devices which suggest some feedback on his part, such as questions immediately followed by answers ("Do demo? Não gloso. Senhor pergunte aos moradores" [10]), and exclamations that indicate the existence of a previous question ("Por que o Governo não cuida?! Ah, eu sei que não é possível. Não me assente o senhor por beócio. Uma coisa é pôr idéias arranjadas, outra é lidar com país de pessoas, de carne e sangue, de mil-e-tantas misérias" [16]).

This situation of duality characterized by the existente of a silent interlocutor, one whose presence is manifested only by the remarks of the narrator and whose speech, if or when existent, is

---

[21] Roberto Schwarz, *"Grande sertão:* a fala," in *A sereia e o desconfiado* (Rio de Janeiro: Civilização Brasileira, 1965), p. 24.

never presented on the pages of the book, might be enough to justify, on a more superficial level, our definition of the technique employed in *Grande sertão: veredas* as a mixture of dialogue and monologue, and the passages just cited would serve to confirm that. However, if we go a little deeper into the subject matter and ask ourselves about the function such a technique takes on in the novel, we will see that these external elements are merely part of a procedure that has been extensively exploited to suggest a perfect adequacy between the content of the narrator's speculation and the form of expressing them – that is, that the questioning which Riobaldo undertakes in his narrative could have reached the point it did only through the use of such a technique, which unites the dialectical structure of the dialogue and the emphasis on a single individual's perspective, characteristic of the monologue.

We have seen while discussing other aspects of *Grande sertão: veredas* that Riobaldo's report is often interrupted by the narrator himself in order to make comments such as: "Eu queria decifrar as coisas que são importantes" (96), "Não tenciono relatar ao senhor minha vida em dobrados passos; servia para que? Quero é armar o ponto dum fato, para depois lhe pedir um conselho" (205-06), or yet "Conto ao senhor é o que eu sei e o senhor não sabe; mas principal quero contar é o que eu não sei se sei, e que pode ser que o senhor saiba" (217). In all these passages, which function as key elements in the novel, the narrator makes explicit the purpose of his narration: the understanding of things that he still has not been able to grasp, and declares that it was for this reason that he sought the aid of his interlocutor, a man who, as he states, "sabe muito, em idéia firme, além de ter carta de doutor" (26). These comments provide two important elements: the fact that Riobaldo's narration is above all a journey to knowledge, or more precisely, a search for self-knowledge and identity, and that this process can be fully achieved only with the aid of another person, or at least with the verbalization permitted by the presence of an interlocutor, however silent.

The fact that Riobaldo's narration is a journey to knowledge can be evidenced here if we refer once again to the theme of the *travessia* in the novel and recall our remark about the existence of two types of crossing which complement each other: a physical or geographical journey which the protagonist undertakes through the backlands and a spiritual or existential crossing which he accomplishes through speech. In the past Riobaldo went through a series of experiences that have left marks on him in the form of questions which disturb him in the present, and he sets himself the task of reporting his life to his interlocutor to obtain anwers for those questions and find thereby some relief for his conscience; thus his narration is an attempt to come to know himself, or rather a constant endeavor to find a meaning for his actions. That is why the narration begins with the word *nonada* and ends with the word *travessia*, two marks that clearly indicate the starting and terminal points of an itinerary which consists, after all, of the configuration of Riobaldo's own existence. Before the beginning of his narration there is nothing but a series of facts and events stored in his mind and a feeling of anguish or guilt whose nature he cannot clearly discern, but at the moment he formulates these things into words – transforms his past into narration – his doubts are gradually dissipated and he attains, as the critic Flávio Loureiro Chaves says, "a unidade e significação de sua experiência."[22] In other words, at the moment in which Riobaldo begins his narration to his interlocutor, he reexperiences his past in a different form, and since a critical distance has been established between himself and those past episodes, he is able to transcend misunderstandings and to find and assume his own identity.

This status as a journey to knowledge confers upon the narrative a dialectical character which is the basis of every true process of knowledge and which can be represented here by the narrator's statement: "Vivendo, se aprende; mas o que se aprende, mais, é só a fazer outras maiores perguntas" (389-90). However, this dialectical process, which consists of a permanent forward movement, resulting from the constant negation of the truths achieved, is totally accomplished in the novel only thanks to the presence of the interlocutor, who if he does not provide the narrator with this element of negation at least provides him with a certain amount of feedback which stimulates the development of his narration. Since Riobaldo does not completely trust his own ability to find answers for the problems which torment him, he seeks the aid of his interlocutor; thus the latter's presence is

---

[22] Flávio Loureiro Chaves, "Perfil de Riobaldo," in *Ficção Latinoamericana* (Porto Alegre: Univ. Federal de Rio Grande do Sul, 1973), p. 126.

indispensable. It is true that the actual dialogue in the novel is that which the protagonist has with himself – that is, a cathartic process of self-revelation in which he becomes his own interlocutor and gradually constucts his personality in the very act of narrating, but since it is only through his social intercourse with the interlocutor that he is able to accomplish this process, the dialogical structure of the narrative is present both in its character of constant evolution and in its etymological sense of a conversation held between two or more persons.

But if on the one hand the elements just mentioned – the dialectical character of the narrative and the importance of the interlocutor's presence – account for a characterization of the technique employed in *Grande sertão: veredas* as a dialogue, on the other we cannot dismiss the idea of its being also a monologue, especially owing to the emphasis put on a single individual's perspective and to the character of flux which the narrative assumes, to the point of making necessary the frequent use of devices to call the reader's attention to the presence of the interlocutor. Although this emphasis on a single indivdual's perspective has been contested by some critics, especially Evelina Hoisel, who in her essay "Elementos dramáticos da estrutura de *Grande sertão: veredas*" mentions the existence in the novel of a plurality of views, or a "polyphony of voices,"[23] it is important to remember that the various views she refers to are filtered through the consciousness of the narrator-protagonist and that what is offered to the interlocutor, and consequently to the reader, is the result of this filtering process – that is, the doubts and anxieties, the constant oscillation which marks the process of growth in which the narrator is involved. This vacillating view, characteristic of Riobaldo, a man divided between two worlds of a different order, is transmitted to the reader, and sets the tone of the entire narrative.

Since the character of flux, to which we have referred, is an element directly associated with the absence of speech on the interlocutor's part and the latter is an aspect upon which we have commented at some length, we will simply mention here that

---

[23] Evelina Hoisel, "Elementos dramáticos da estrutura de *Grande sertão: veredas*," *Minas Gerais* [Belo Horizonte], 29 January 1977, Supl. Lit. p. 6.

this element can easily be seen in the way the novel is constructed, which has been described by the critic Augusto de Campos in his now-classic essay "Um lance de 'dés' do *Grande sertão*," as "um fluxo contínuo, sem pausa, um só fôlego riocorrente."[24] This sole, continuous flux is suggested, in its formal, external aspect, by the lack of a division into chapters and the existence of extensive paragraphs; and in its development even the pauses existing in the actual scenes with the interlocutor – let us not forget that Riobaldo's narration lasts for three days, the time spent by the interlocutor at his farm as his guest – are indicated merely by brief and subtle remarks often unnoticed by the reader, such as: "Vai assim, vem outro café, se pita um bom cigarro" (292). With this flux Riobaldo accomplishes his existential crossing – a dialogue with himself, a dialectical process of self-knowledge or revelation which brings him to an encounter with his own self, or rather to the discovery of his own identity. But before we conclude our presentation of these elements responsible for conferring upon Riobaldo's narrative a monological character, let us point out that such a character is suggested by the protagonist himself in the following passage, where, after blaming himself for having confessed to the interlocutor his feelings toward Diadorim, he declares: "O senhor é de fora, meu amigo mas meu estranho. Mas, talvez por isto mesmo. Falar com estranho assim, que bem ouve e logo longe se vai embora, é um segundo proveito: faz do jeito que eu falasse mais mesmo comigo" (39).

By describing the elements which characterize the technique employed in *Grande sertão: veredas* as a dialogue-monologue, we have automatically made evident the fact that this technique is particularly appropriate to express the content of the narrative. This appropriateness, which can be exemplified by the parallels established between Riobaldo's search for self-knowledge and the dialectical structure of the dialogue, or between the fact that the narrator constitutes his own interlocutor and the emphasis on a single individual's perspective, is made even more obvious if we reflect that such a technique stresses the identification between the protagonist's existential quest and his quest for a new language by

---

[24] Augusto de Campos, "Um lance de 'dés' do *Grande sertão*," *Revista do Livro*, 4, No. 16 (December 1959), 48.

revealing that the former can be accomplished only by means of the latter – that it is only through language, through social intercourse or the communication with his fellow men – that the individual can find his own identity and attain a certain state of self-gratification. However, if all these aspects indicate the choice of a suitable technique, in great part responsible for the structural harmony of the novel, the use of such a technique has also some implications which transcend the structure of the novel and reflect the principles of an entire aesthetic program which aims at opening up new pathways for contemporary Latin American fiction.

This opening up of new pathways, resulting from the use of a hybrid technique which mixes dialogue and monologue, has not gone unnoticed by the critics of Guimarães Rosa, in particular Nelly Novaes Coelho, who states that "De acordo com a abertura do 'eu' para o 'nós' que é iniciada pela ficção contemporânea, o processo do 'monólogo interior' (que fecha a personagem no círculo de sua própria experiência, em sondagens introspectivas) amplia-se no 'estilo dialogante' ou 'interrogativo' (um 'eu' que se dirige a um 'tu' que permanece fora da narrativa) – estilo que abre para o narrador o espaço da reflexão e da liberdade criadora."[25] However, if on the one hand the critic has correctly observed the contribution brought about by Rosa's replacement in *Grande sertão: veredas* of the pure interior monologue – a form so much explored by contemporary fiction and which, as she points out, encloses the character into the circle of his own experience – by what she designates as *estilo dialogante* – a form that opens up for the narrator a space for reflection and freedom of creation – on the other hand she has gone no further than that and has failed to indicate the importance such a technique assumes as an expression of Rosa's world view.

It is true that by abandoning the pure interior monologue Guimarães Rosa transcended the excessive subjectivism so much criticized, especially by Marxist-oriented scholars, in the works of his contemporaries – particularly European and North American novelists – and moved a step forward as regards the craft of the genre, but the consequences of his use of a hybrid technique are

---

[25] Nelly Novaes Coelho, "A arte narrativa e o espírito lúdico de Guimarães Rosa," *O Estado de São Paulo*, 14 April 1974, Supl. Lit., p. 1.

not restricted to that. By preserving some of the aspects characteristic of the interior monologue, the author enables the reader to accompany more closely and with greater intensity the conflicts of the narrator-protagonist, and also paradoxically contributes to the dialectical continuity of the narrative, by permitting greater identification between the reader and the interlocutor, who, through his silence, is transformed into a kind of projection of the reader himself. Furthermore, by making use of a dialogical situation and at the same time dispensing with the traditional form of the dialogue, or rather with an essentially dramatic technique, Guimarães Rosa abandons the didactic tone usually present in such works (in which the narrator and his interlocutor are mirror images of the author himself) but maintains, on the other hand, the element of social interchange characteristic of the Platonic dialogue, whose basic purpose consists of inciting and promoting the constant search for truth. And finally, by using the structure of a dialogue, he not only strives to keep the interlocutor and reader awake and alert but, especially, calls the latter's attention to the vital relationship between man and his power of speech, thereby revitalizing the oral tradition in literature.[26]

4.4. "Grande sertão: veredas": an Epic, Lyrical and Dramatic Work

These aspects, all resulting from the use of the dialogue-monologue technique, indicate by their character of nonexclusiveness the tendency toward a synthesis of opposing elements which characterizes the author's work, and consequently reflect the importance of this hybrid technique as the exspression of a world view based on the belief that relativity is the only possible way of approaching reality. But since this technique, so properly employed in *Grande sertão: veredas,* can be fully understood only when seen in its relationship with other elements of the novel, also marked by hybridism, which play a significant role as expressions of the author's world view, we will take a look at these elements now, and start by specifying them as the fusion of the traditional genres

---

[26] This fact has been observed by the critic Elizabeth Lowe, in "Dialogues of *Grande sertão: veredas,*" *Luso-Brazilian Review,* 13 (Winter 1976), 231-43.

of literature – the epic, the lyric, and the dramatic – and the mixture of realism and imagination.

The first of these elements, so intimately connected with the technique just discussed – the fusion of the traditional genres – is one of the aspects of Rosa's novel that have most occupied his critics, who have often engaged in long polemics in an attempt to classify the work in one of the above modalities. However, in spite of these polemics (and the existence of a few brilliant theses directed toward a definition of the book as a "Faustian drama" or a "modern version of the romance of chivalry,") the majority of these critics seem to have concluded that *Grande sertão: veredas* can be seen only as a kind of "mixed genre" in which those elements that traditionally characterize each of the modalities mentioned coexist in perfect harmony, constituting different levels of the narrative which complement one another. This position, already implicit though in an unconscious manner in Proença's division of the novel into three levels[27] and later expressed by Schwarz, who reduces the levels to two (*"Grande sertão:* a fala," pp. 24-25), finds a clear formulation in Hoisel's essay cited above, in which the author, after endorsing Schwarz's division, affirms:

> É do jogo relacional e textual do plano 1 – diálogo-monólogo dramático – com o plano 2 – curso épico das aventuras, enformados pelo lirismo que *Grande sertão: veredas* se constrói como uma forma altamente híbrida e mista, que impõe as leis de sua própria composição e não se deixa classificar por nenhuma categoria literária. Decidir se *Grande sertão: veredas* pertence *ou* ao gênero épico, *ou* dramático, *ou* lírico, resultará sempre numa falsa colocação, na medida em que é simultaneamente épico-dramático-lírico, autopostulando-se, assim, como elemento indecidível, que não se deixa compreender nem reduzir a marcas decidíveis, a polaridades delimitadas. ("Elementos dramáticos," p. 6)

---

[27] In *Trilhas no Grande sertão,* Proença speaks of the existence in *Grande sertão: veredas* of a "superposition of levels," which he divides into three parts: "A primeira, individual, subjetiva, ... antagonismo entre os elementos da alma humana; a segunda, coletiva, ... influenciada pela literatura popular que faz do cangaceiro Riobaldo um símile de herói medieval, retirado de romance de cavalaria e aculturado nos sertões do Brasil Central; a terceira, telúrica, mítica, em que os elementos naturais – sertão, vento, rio, buritis – se tornam personagens vivos e atuantes" (pp. 9-10).

Since scholars have already made exhaustive listings of the elements accounting for the inclusion of *Grande sertão: veredas* in the realm of the epic, the lyric, and the dramatic, we will not discuss this issue in detail here, but we will mention some of the most significant of these elements because of their importance for the understanding of the novel as a whole. However, it is first important to observe that if their presence indicates on the one hand a kinship between Rosa's book and the paradigms of the genres mentioned, on the other hand they are so frequently employed in a manner different from that found in such paradigms that they hardly if ever stand as arguments for a classification; they may often even serve a kind of parodic function which can be said to question the exclusive character of each of these genres. Based on this observation about the way these elements are used in Rosa's novel we can state at this point that the book is a "critical synthesis" of all these traditional forms.

The epic elements present in *Grande sertão: veredas* are, of course, concentrated in what we have designated as the line of the past – especially in its objective modality – and correspond to Riobaldo's experiences as a jagunço – that is, his battles and toils in the backlands, and the episodes which characterize the jagunço's way of life. Most of these episodes and events, all marked by a grandiloquent tone, are meticulously described and serve, in the majority of cases, the function of exalting the qualities of the jagunços – their bravery, nobleness, and sense of honor and loyalty – and the worthiness of their war, which consists of an honorable effort to maintain the way of life prevalent in the universe they inhabit. The jagunços are, as we have seen, endowed in *Grande sertão: veredas* with a great deal of idealism, bringing them very close to the heroes of the chivalric romance, and their war is presented, especially in the second phase (after the treason), as the fight for a noble cause or, more appropriately, the quest for a sacred goal; this aspect confers upon it a magnitude characteristic of the epic genre.

The elements must cited – the heroic, idealistic side of the jagunços (which can be exemplified by the protagonist himself, imbued above all with a noble character and a strong sense of justice and responsibility, and the portrayal of the jagunços' leaders, most especially Joca Ramiro and Medeiro Vaz) and the magnitude of the war in which they are engaged – would be enough to show the presence of an epic tradition in the corpus of *Grande sertão: veredas*. Moving from the generic to the specific, however, we consider it worthwhile to mention a few episodes which are primarily distinguished by the predominance of an epic tone. For example, Zé Bebelo's trial, which Proença has defined as an extract from a romance of chivalry transplanted to the Brazilian backlands; the announcement of Joca Ramiro's death, which causes the break-up of the jagunço group; the crossing of the Liso do Sussuarão under Riobaldo's leadership; the siege at the Tucanos farm and the detailed description of the final battle, preceded by the enumeration of the combatants' names; and finally the pact with the devil, which has often been compared to the descent to the underworld, where the heroes of Classical epic poems seek courage and strength to be able to confront the forces of evil.

But our characterization of the epic elements in *Grande sertão: veredas* would be incomplete without mention of a few formal traits, such as the number of secondary stories embedded in the narrative, and the chronology of the main story – the story of Riobaldo's life as a jagunço – which begins *in media res*. Furthermore, it is indispensable to mention the main female figures of the novel – Otacília, Nhorinhá, and Diadorim – who form a kind of mythical triad, composed of the opposition spirit vs. flesh and of a third possibility that could very plausibly be seen as a fusion of the two preceding terms. Otacília is the pure maid, the platonic beauty indispensable in the chivalric romance, the figure who inspires the knight, and the prize he receives after he overcomes all his tribulations; Nhorinhá, the prostitute, is the embodiment of carnal love, the sweet touch of Eros that Riobaldo received in a backland oasis and which he nourishes in his mind for the rest of his life; and finally Diadorim, the woman disguised as a warrior of the Classical and Medieval tradition, is the synthesis of these two kinds of love, the ambiguous, mysterious figure who embodies through her androgyny all the contradictory forces which illuminate and gratify man but at the same time push him into the abyss of his own existence.

Unlike the epic elements of *Grande sertão: veredas*, which are associated with Riobaldo's physical or geographical crossing of the sertão, the dramatic character of the novel is intimately connected with the protagonist's existential crossing and consequently with his search for a new language; thus it is centered upon the line we have designated here as that of the present, both in its speculative and in its metalinguistic modalities. It is on this line, which has itself the structure of a drama in that it is constructed, as we have seen, by a dialogical situation between the narrator-protagonist and a silent interlocutor, that the central tension of the novel lies – the doubts Riobaldo has concerning the existence or nonexistence of the devil and his attempt to express these doubts through the medium of language. Just like every true character of drama, Riobaldo constructs his own personality by means of his speech, and since this process is accomplished only in the session with his interlocutor, the space of this narrative line takes on the proportions of a theater stage where the drama of an existence is represented. This has caused some critics to see Rosa's novel as a kind of drama and to point out frequent parallels between it and some of the great Western paradigms of the genre.

But if the dramatic elements present in *Grande sertão: veredas* are mostly concentrated on the level of the present, that does not mean that they are exclusively restricted to this level, for the whole novel is constructed in an alternating manner which clearly indicates the tension/relaxation movement that characterizes drama. Evelina Hoisel has shown how dramatic tension is present in some of the novel's passages which are predominantly marked by an epic tone, such as the battles, and also in the inner conflicts the protagonist experiences while marching through the backlands. Hoisel also enumerates a series of other elements, also typical of drama, which play an important role in the structure of *Grande sertão: veredas* ("Elementos dramáticos," passim). Among these it is worthwhile to mention the pathos which forces Riobaldo to act, thus guaranteeing successful vengeance; the series of ritualistic ceremonies, such as Zé Bebelo's trial, the pact with the devil, and the first meeting with Diadorim at the edge of the de-Janeiro river; and finally the metaphor of the theater, so frequently employed, in passages such as: "Vida devia de ser como na sala do teatro, cada um inteiro fazendo com forte gosto seu papel, desempenho" (232); "O teatral do mundo: um de estadela, os outros ensinados, calados" (345); and "Meu corpo gostava de Diadorim. . . . Meu corpo gostava do corpo dele, na sala do teatro" (173). All these elements, as well as other less important ones, strongly contribute to an intense dramatic atmosphere, but it is above all through the convergence of the narration of Riobaldo's past experiences with his reexperiencing of that past in the present that the dramatic unity of *Grande sertão: veredas* is constructed and established.

The lyrical character in *Grande sertão: veredas* is to a large extent associated with the use of a first-person narrator, and can be more easily felt in the narrative sublines which are predominantly marked by a great deal of subjectivism, namely the subjective modality of the line of the past, composed of Riobaldo's inner conflicts while a jagunço, and the speculative modality of the line of the present, in which the protagonist accomplishes his existential crossing of the sertão. Here, though, it is important to observe that since the entire narrative is filtered through the consciousness of Riobaldo, who reexperiences his past life in the act of narration, the whole universe evoked is presented as an undivided unity, and the distinction between past and present becomes fluid and indefinable. Thus, if some of the most lyrical scenes of the entire novel can be said to form part of the subjective subline of the past because of their having occurred in the period of Riobaldo's life as a jagunço, it is important to remember that they are being evoked in the present and that the lyrical tone which marks them so intensely is an effect of the narrator's cathartic process of self-revelation, expressed through language in the presence of his interlocutor. These scenes are, for example, those containing a description of the landscape of the sertão, which Riobaldo learned to appreciate after his contact with Diadorim, and the passages in which he narrates the pleasant moments spent in the backlands in the company of his friend.

These frequent scenes, as well as a series of others in which the narrator evokes his feelings toward Otacília and Nhorinhá, are passages of great beauty and sensitivity which reveal the presence of a strong lyrical component in the corpus of *Grande sertão: veredas*. But again, as in the case of the genres previously studied, the lyrical character of the narrative is not restricted to such passages. Proença dedicated a section of *Trilhas no Grande sertão* to the study of the role of the natural elements in the novel, particularly the river, the sertão, the wind, and the *buriti* palm tree, which he considers essentially lyrical, but it is undoubtedly in the formal aspects of the narrative, most especially in language itself, that the presence of this lyrical component becomes most obvious.

In his essay "Canto e plumagem das palavras," in which he makes a detailed analysis of some of the basic linguistic innovations introduced by Guimarães Rosa in his works, Oswaldino Marques places the author's narratives under the categories of both prose and poetry and defines his style with the word *prosoema*, a neologism which indicates the fusion of the two modalities (*prosa* "prose" and *poema* "poem").[28] This view, which has been shared by several other critics of Brazilian literature, among them Pedro Xisto and Franklin de Oliveira, who have produced long essays on the subject, derives from the fact that Guimarães Rosa, though having written his works in a discourse-like, syntagmatic manner, typical of prose writing, produced a creative kind of expression, which is, according to Herbert Read, the very element which characterizes poetic activity.[29] In Rosa's narratives, particularly in *Grande Sertão: veredas*, the word, is always employed as something new or original, stripped of all its worn-out elements; it generates a highly lyrical text, marked by a predominance of the poetic function of revelation.

But if these two elements – the process of condensation according to which the word always suggests more than the simple concept of the object represented by the signifier, and the character of originality, which consists of the creation or re-creation of the word at the moment of expression – per se indicate the lyrical nature of Guimarães Rosa's narrative language, it is also worthwhile to register here the abundant use made by the author of a series of devices which, though not exclusively characteristic of lyrical poetry, strongly contribute to his language. These devices, which the American scholar Mary Daniel has carefully studied,[30] range from the simple use of rhythmical elements such as asson-

---

[28] Oswaldino Marques, "Canto e plumagem das palavras," in *Ensaios escolhidos* (Rio de Janeiro: Civilização Brasileira, 1968), pp. 82-83.
[29] Herbert Read, *English Prose Style* (London: G. Bell & Sons, 1956); critic Read makes the following statement about the distinction between prose and poetry: "The distinction between Poetry and Prose is not and never can be a formal one... it is a psychological distinction. Poetry is the expression of one form of mental activity, Prose is the expression of another form. Poetry is creative expression: Prose is constructive expression.... Poetry seems to be generated in the process of condensation; Prose in the process of dispersion" (p. x).
[30] Mary Daniel, *João Guimarães Rosa – travessia literária* (Rio de Janeiro: José Olympio, 1968).

ance, alliteration, and rhyme to the inclusion of entire poems and folk songs, usually marked by a very cadenced rhythmical pattern. One of the most significant examples of the use of these elements in *Grande sertão: veredas* is the song of Siruiz, which Riobaldo once heard from a jagunço and which becomes in the novel a symbol of all poetry that man pursues in his life.[31]

All these elements cited, in addition to the structural organization of the novel, which is essentially musical, characterized, as the critic Óscar Lopes says, by the recurrence of certain themes which "se definem, enlaçam e periodicamente se opõem, de novo, enriquecidos com as relações recíprocas,"[32] make it perfectly plausible to state, as have several of Rosa's critics, that *Grande sertão: veredas* is a novel marked by a significant lyrical component which neutralizes the distinction, already weakened in previous Latin American literature, between prose and poetry.

Before concluding our discussion about the fusion of the epic, the lyric, and the dramatic in the corpus of *Grande sertão: veredas*, let us go back for a while to our statement about the parodic manner in which some of the elements mentioned as characteristic of each of these genres are employed in Rosa's novel in order to see in what way the book can be said to consist of a "critical synthesis" of all these traditional genres. We have noted, for example, in connection with the epic, that one of the elements that account for the inclusion of the book in the realm of this genre is the exaltation of the jagunços' qualities and of the worthiness of their war, which is viewed as a kind of sacred duty from which they cannot escape These elements, however, though definitely present in the novel, are not treated in the same manner as they are in the Classical epic poem or in the medieval romance of chivalry. Far from being exclusively heroes, the jagunços of *Grande sertão: veredas* are also a group of social outcasts, struggling to maintain a system

---

[31] Riobaldo first heard the song of Siruiz when he was an adolescent, living at his godfather's farm (114). From that moment on, the song is recalled by him, frequently with the words changed, at different moments of his life. The meaning of the song in the novel is multiple, and it is beyond our purpose to exploit its several possibilities at this point; however, it is worthwhile to mention that it is associated with the protagonist's process of learning on both levels of the narrative (past and present).

[32] Oscar Lopes, "Guimarães Rosa," *Seara Nova* [Lisbon], No. 1425 (July 1964).

that marginalizes them, and exploited by the wealthy landowners. The protagonist, Riobaldo, unlike the Classical heroes, is a typical example of a split personality, a man who is indecisive throughout the entire novel and never accepts definitively the function of a jagunço. Contrary to what is expected of an epic hero or a medieval knight, our protagonist is frequently dominated by fear and comes to the point of fainting in two decisive moments of the narrative – the pact and the final battle – discarding the chance to clarify the doubts which tormented him. He is, like D. Quixote, a parodic figure in this sense, but here also, as in the former case, a distinction must be made: whereas D. Quixote can be said to constitute, as stated by the critic Wilson Martins in his preface to Mary Daniel's book, "o verdadeiro cavaleiro... vivendo aventuras imaginárias," Riobaldo is "o falso cavaleiro envolvido em aventuras verdadeiras" (Daniel, p. xx).

In the same way that the jagunços, in spite of their heroic side, are also portrayed in the novel in a manner that indicates a demythification of the purely idealistic types of the Classical and medieval literary tradition, the war represented therein, in spite of its presentation as serving a noble cause, also undergoes a process of demythification in the sense that it is seen as something useless and alienating which, far from bringing any sort of satisfaction to man, drives him, on the contrary, to misery and further disgust. Motivated by an alien cause – the love for his friend Diadorim – which is not directly associated with the vendetta, Riobaldo is engaged in a war, and at the end he is victorious insofar as the war itself is concerned, but he loses that very object which constituted his reason for fighting: Diadorim is killed in the final combat and Riobaldo, now the image of a frustrated hero (hence the etymology of his name, which Proença explained as being composed of *rio* "river" and *baldo* "lacking, missing, wanting, useless," indicating a river that, like the Urucúia with which he is often identified, flows into another river rather than into the ocean), is condemned to a guilty feeling which he will carry for the rest of his life. This demythification of the war, which is made evident, for example, every time the narrator questions the necessity of a certain combat, is also present in the descriptions of the battles, all marked by a strong emphasis on violence, and of scenes of the jagunços' everyday life, such as those at Hermógenes' camp, where cruelty and sadism constitute the very theme.[33]

The use of lyrical elements in a manner different from that within which they are generally found in the paradigms of the genre can be exemplified in *Grande sertão: veredas* by the fact that the past, far from being approached from a purely nostalgic perspective, is focused on by the narrator in critical terms, and is reconstituted not as a source of pleasure to Riobaldo but rather to clarify the doubts he has about the existence of the devil, to attain, as a consequence, his identity in the world. It is true that the nostalgic tone is present several times in the narrative, especially in the passages mentioned in which he recollects his emotional experiences with Otacília, Nhorinhá, and particularly Diadorim. But since these recollections are all subordinated in the novel to the intellectual function of investigation, for which he seeks the aid of his interlocutor, the lyrical tone they contain is associated with a critical view of his past which sets up a certain distance between the subject and the objects evoked.

Another aspect which can also serve as an example of the particular manner in which the lyrical elements are treated in *Grande sertão: veredas* is that it contains a love story which on the one hand is typical and on the other is a negation of the model characteristic of the traditional stories of this sort. The story of the relationship between Riobaldo and Diadorim can be considered a typical love story in that it presents, as Jean-Paul Bruyas says, "os mais profundos temas como os mais fúteis: enraizamento longínquo da paixão nas fronteiras da infância...; persistência dessa paixão, apesar de (por causa de?) um obstáculo invencível...; amor que orienta toda uma vida e a deixa vazia quando o objeto deste amor morre; delicadezas, ciúmes, briguinhas – até que num olhar *a alma* se manifeste de novo e firme uma vez mais a aliança."[34] But it is also a negation of this kind of story, owing, among other reasons, to the fact that their love is always subordinated to the opposition between appearance and reality and is

---

[33] These descriptions led the critic Antônio Houaiss, in an interview in the magazine *José* (November-December 1976, pp. 18-31), to declare that the author of *Grande sertão: veredas* approaches violence in an almost documentary manner and thus offers a critical view of the so-called "ideology of nonviolence" which has for so long been seen by Brazilian intellectuals as a trait of their country's history.

[34] Jean-Paul Bruyas, "Técnicas, estruturas e visão em *Grande sertão: veredas*," *Revista do Instituto de Estudos Brasileiros* [Universidade de São Paulo], No. 18 (1976), p. 80.

submitted, on the level of the narrator's speculations, to the process of questioning which directs the entire narrative and reduces it at the end to a mere shadow. In Bruyas's words, "Esta paixão nunca é analisada [como nos modelos tradicionais do gênero], nunca atinge para o leitor, a forma superior de existência de algo que é explicado (desenrolado diante dos olhos... como um rolo de pergaminho); é lançada, como um fato bruto; para nós, e de modo especial para aquele que o vive, aos vinte anos, para aquele que se lembra trinta anos mais tarde de ter vivido aquilo: uma realidade opaca, intacta, de pedregulho" (ibid., p. 85).

Since the use of dramatic elements in a manner different from that in which they appear in the models of the genre has already been made evident when we discussed the technique employed in *Grande sertão: veredas,* according to which the dialogue, essential in the drama, is reduced to what Schwarz has defined as "dialogo pela metade ou diálogo visto por uma face" ("*Grande sertão:* a fala," p. 24), and is also associated with the opposition between realism and imagination that will occupy us in the following paragraphs, we will limit ourselves at this point to a brief mention of a device, intimately connected with this latter opposition, which is the critical distancing, so much employed by Brecht in his works, and which plays a relevant role in the corpus of Rosa's novel. This device, which consists of breaking the illusion created by the theater (or by art in general) by means of the frequent inclusion into the text of comments, judgments, or remarks that indicate the presence of the narrator, is an element of the structure of *Grande sertão: veredas,* which contains an entire subline that we have called metalinguistic; and it is thanks in great part to the use of such an element that the narrator is given the possibility of questioning not only his whole life as a jagunço but also the very act of narrating and the technique employed for his narration. In Rosa's novel, the narrator, to cite Bruyas once again, refuses "atingir o leitor por processos ilusionistas, tentando dar a impressão de que ele se acha diante da própria vida" ("Técnicas," p. 81), and establishes, as a result, a highly critical perspective which induces the reader to think and to take part in his journey through words. Thus, if on the one hand the narrator makes use, as we have previously shown, of a series of dramatic elements which might give his reader the impression of being a spectator at a performance, on the other he breaks with this illusion and produces a mixed kind of work which is, above all, critical, in the deepest sense of the word.

4.5. The Real and the Imaginary in the Universe of "Grande sertão: veredas"

4.5.1. Story vs. History

The other hybrid element of *Grande sertão: veredas* which will concern us here – the fusion of realism and imagination – is an important aspect at this point of our discussion because it is intimately connected with the neutralization of the opposition with which we have been dealing in this chapter, namely the traditional opposition, existing in the works of earlier Latin American novelists, between aestheticism and social commitment. Thus in our approach to the issue we will focus first on the neutralization of the opposition per se, and will later attempt to trace the relationship which exists between this aspect and the fusion of an aesthetic consciousness with the question of social commitment. However, since the neutralization of the opposition between realism and imagination is an aspect also present in the language stricto sensu employed in the novel, we will approach this issue from a double perspective too – that is, first in general and second specifically in relation to language – and will see how this fact has contributed to confer upon *Grande setão: veredas* the character of a "synthesis" novel.

We have seen when discussing Riobaldo's status as a jagunço and the view of the sertão offered in *Grande sertão: veredas* that Guimarães Rosa starts the process of representing reality from concrete elements – the jagunço who inhabits the Brazilian backlands and the physical or geographical region which constitutes his environment – and that he transforms or re-creates these elements to form the universe of his novel. However, we have also observed that in his process of transformation or re-creation of the material selected from actual life the author never loses track completely of that reality which served as point of departure, and builds up a kind of novel that is, at the same time, "o mais profundo e mais completo estudo até hoje feito sobre a plebe rural brasileira" and "a mais profunda e completa idealização desta mesma plebe" (*As formas do falso*, p. 74).

The fact that Guimarães Rosa transformed or re-created in his novel elements extracted from actual life without losing track of the objective traits which characterize them indicates a consciousness on his part that art imitates life not by photographing it but, as Franklin de Oliveira says in his essay on Rosa for *A literatura no Brasil*, "agindo por processos idênticos – criando formas mentais como o universo físico cria formas naturais."[35] Guimarães Rosa is conscious that art is not and never can be a copy of reality, a photographic reproduction of what exists in real life, but rather that it constitutes a fictitious representation of such a life; thus he does not hesitate to give free rein to his imagination, and creates, as Cândido affirms, "sobre o fato concreto e verificável da jagunçagem... um romance de cavalaria" (*TA*, p. 129) in which historical reality is mixed with a great deal of legend.

This fusion of history with story – that is, the mixture of elements extracted from the Brazilian backlands with others deriving from the medieval romance of chivalry – was not an arbitrary choice, and at this point we can affirm, as Galvão did, that "a presença de elementos do imaginário da cavalaria no *Grande sertão: veredas*... não é apenas algo de proposto com o objetivo de dignificar a matéria e operar uma contribuição a mais para a mitologia do cangaço" (*As formas do falso*, p. 52). We have seen in the first section of this study that, for the authors of Latin America's "new narrative," the work of art has a reality of its own which cannot be subordinated to the reality of the outside world, but also that it is not an isolated phenomenon which exists in a void; on the contrary, the work exists in a context, the world of its author. Thus if we examine the context which served Guimarães Rosa as point of departure – the Brazilian sertão – we will easily see that the elements which form the material of a chivalric romance are neither imposed from the outside nor deriving exclusively from the author's erudite knowledge, but rather an aspect which constitutes an integral part of the mental complex of the man from the sertão.

---

[35] Franklin de Oliveira, "Guimarães Rosa," in *A literatura no Brasil*, ed. Afrânio Coutinho, 2d ed., V: *Modernismo* (Rio de Janeiro: Editorial Sul Americana, 1970), p. 406.

The men from the sertão, says Rosa in his interview with Lorenz, are "fabulistas por naturaleza," and he continues:

> El narrar cuentos lo llevamos en la sangre. Ya en la cuna recibimos ese don para toda la vida. Desde pequeños escuchamos constantemente las narraciones multicolores contadas por los viejos, los cuentos y leyendas y, finalmente, nos creamos un mundo que nos semeja una leyenda cruel. De este modo uno se habitúa. Y el hecho de narrar cuentos corre por nuestras venas y nos penetra en el cuerpo y en el alma, pues el Sertão es el alma de sus hombres. . . . [Yo] tenía siempre los oídos atentos, escuchaba todo lo que podía y comencé a trasformar el ambiente que me rodeaba en leyenda, porque éste, en su esencia, era y sigue siendo una leyenda. (Lorenz, "Diálogo," p. 31)

In this world which was, and continues to be a legend, in this magic kind of universe where fantasy is an element of people's daily lives, the stories belonging to the medieval chivalric romance, which had been transmitted orally from one generation to another, had been incorporated by people and become a part of their collective consciousness. Thus, when Rosa makes use of this material in his novel, he is not introducing any element alien to the context selected, but rather simply utilizing the same procedure employed by popular singers and storytellers, who in their compositions mix those elements with actual events.

The idealized world of chivalry is an integral part of the consciousness of the backlands man, and since in Rosa's works the latter is the pivotal element, rather than the landscape, there is nothing strange in the fact that the sertão is often portrayed in the novel from a chivalric perspective. Besides, the narrator-protagonist of *Grande sertão: veredas* is a man from the sertão, who posesses a mythical-sacred consciousness; thus, there is no unlikeliness in the fact that he frequently refers to his own life in terms of a chivalric romance. On the contrary, the elements of such a genre are a significant part of the fanciful present in his daily life; they are something which is experienced by him at every moment; thus nothing is more appropriate than this aspect to express this side of his consciousness. In representing the sertão in *Grande sertão: veredas,* Rosa also offered a picture of its fanciful aspect; in so doing he was paradoxically a realist in the sense that he approached reality from a multiple perspective. He was a realist in the sense in which we have been employing the term in this study – that is, one who tries to embrace reality in as many of its aspects as possible.

At this point it is important to observe, however, that this notion of "total" realism can be fully understood only if we realize that the two elements – the inner and the outer world, the natural and the fanciful sertão – are inseparable in the novel, forming one sole block, which is the universe represented. The fanciful aspect of the sertão is not isolated, dissociated from the natural one; thus, in the same way that the choice of chivalric elements to represent that aspect does not come from a purely arbitrary attitude on the author's part but rather from experience and familiarity with the context re-created, the presence of these elements in the mind of the backlands man is neither a mere accident nor something simply deriving from an oral cultural tradition. Although this observation might seem at first glance extraneous to the literary fact, it becomes a crucial issue in any approach to *Grande sertão: veredas* when we see that the existence of such a tradition, fundamental as it may be, does not by itself justify the parallel established in the novel between the jagunços' world and that of the romance of chivalry. This tradition found a fertile ground in the Brazilian backlands owing in great part to similarities existing between the structure of that society and that of the European Middle Ages.

The similarities between the feudal structure of medieval European society and that of the Brazilian sertão at the time the story of Riobaldo is supposed to have occurred (late nineteenth or early twentieth century) were pointed out by Antônio Cândido first in his essay "O sertão e o mundo" and later in "O homem dos avessos," in which, after analyzing the jagunços' behavior in *Grande sertão: veredas*, he concludes: "A conduta real os aproxima bastante do cavaleiro como realmente existiu, e que foi, afinal de contas, um jagunço ao seu modo, desempenhando função parecida numa sociedade sem poder central forte, baseada, como a do Sertão, na competição dos grupos rurais" (*TA*, p. 130). Although the critic's argument does not go much beyond that, the kinship which he points out between the two forms of society and between the role of the jagunço and that of the knight in their respective environments suffices to evidence the relationship existing in the novel between the external world of the sertão and its fanciful side. In this world, characterized like the medieval one by a radical division between landowners and liege men, a world in which the jagunço, though not belonging to either of these opposed classes, is dependent on the former for his own survival, fantasy is the only possible way out for him. Thus, like his counterpart (also an outcast in his own way), he transforms his life into an adventure and equates reality with fantasy. The result is that fantasy becomes a part of his daily life, and the barrier which might possibly exist between the two categories disappears.

This relationship between the external world of the sertão and its imaginary side is a fundamental aspect of *Grande sertão: veredas* not only because it reveals the existence of a harmony between the novel's component elements, and consequently contributes to its inner coherence, but also because it points, better perhaps than any other aspect of the narrative, to the parallel existing between the universe re-created and that which served the author as point of departure. These universes are both characterized by a reversibility of the real and the fanciful, and the presence of this common denominator between them has an important consequence as regards the neutralization of the opposition between history and story. For if it is true that the former is consciously transformed in *Grande sertão: veredas* to serve the author's creative purposes, the story also contains a great amount of history; and since the same process of transformation which takes place in relation to art is accomplished in real life by those belonging to the context that served the author as point of departure, it becomes difficult to trace a neat barrier separating one thing from the other, and the opposition previously existing between history and story fades away. It is the neutralization of such an opposition which constitutes the theme of the story, embedded in Riobaldo's narrative, about the pact established by Davidão and Faustino, and it is also to the same thing that the narrator often refers in passages such as "Tem horas em que penso que a gente carecia, de repente, de acordar de alguma espécie de encanto. As pessoas, e as coisas, não são de verdade" (81) or "Nas estórias, nos livros, não é desse jeito?" (154).

4.5.2. A "Synthesis" Type of Language

Having seen how the opposition between realism and imagination is neutralized, in general terms, in the corpus of *Grande sertão: veredas*, we will now take a brief look at the way this neutralization is effected by the type of language employed in the novel. We will begin by recalling that the latter is an aesthetic creation, composed of the fusion of elements deriving from experience and observation with others entirely invented at the very moment of expression. The type of language employed by Guimarães Rosa in his works, though based to some extent on the model spoken in the Brazilian backlands, is not the faithful reproduction of any actual dialect existing in the country, but rather an aesthetic synthesis, and as such it embodies the elimination of the opposition we have been discussing here. To see how this elimination is actually accomplished as a result of the "synthesis" character of the type of language used, we will show how this synthesis is constituted and in what way it is appropriate to express the author's concept of reality and its representation through art.

Guimarães Rosa wrote his works in Brazilian Portuguese, a language that has assimilated a great number of elements from the languages of the Indians and Africans who have contributed significantly to the country's cultural complex. But it is important to keep in mind that in his use of such a language he did not limit himself to any specific dialect spoken in Brazil. Rather, he utilized a series of elements or devices originating in the most varied regions of the country, and to all this he added not only a number of contributions borrowed from foreign languages or revitalized from Old Portuguese, but also elements which he himself created, by exploring the possibilities present within the system of this language. Thus, to the synthesis already existing – that is, the Portuguese spoken in Brazil – he added his own synthesis, which he defines when he affirms: "Eu quero tudo: o mineiro, o brasileiro, o português, o latim – talvez até o esquimó e o tártaro,"[36] and later explains, in his interview with Lorenz:

---

[36] Rosa's statement was cited by Wilson Martins, in "Jõe Guimarró," *O Estado de São Paulo*, 8 May 1965, Supl. Lit., p. 2.

> [Incluyo] en mi dicción ciertas singularidades dialécticas de mi región, que no son lenguaje literario pero llevan su marca original, no están gastadas y casi siempre son de una gran sabiduría idiomática. Aparte, como autor del siglo XX, debo ocuparme del idioma formado bajo la influencia de las ciencias modernas y que representan una especie de dialecto. Además, está a mi disposición ese magnífico idioma ya casi olvidado: el antiguo portugués de los hombres sabios, de los poetas de entonces, de los escolásticos de la Edad Media, tal como se hablaba en Coimbra, etc. Habría todavía mucho que mencionar, pero nos llevaría demasiado lejos. En todos los casos tengo que componer todo esto, yo diría "compensar," y así nace entonces mi idioma que, quiero dejarlo bien sentado, está fundido con elementos que no son de mi propiedad particular, sino que son accesibles a todos los demás. (Lorenz, p. 38)

This linguistic synthesis accomplished by Guimarães Rosa – a feat that has no precedents in the history of Latin American fiction – expresses, in a wide and coherent manner, the world view the author intends to represent. Guimarães Rosa is conscious of the fact – it is never superfluous to insist on this point – that in art imitating is not copying but rather creating, or, as Eduardo Portella states in an article, on *Grande sertão: veredas*, that "a dependência com respeito à natureza é uma dependência livre,"[37] and he uses a type of language in accordance with this view, that is, one that could be defined as a consciously aesthetic creation.

This aesthetic consciousness that Rosa reveals through his choice of language seems, however, not to have been understood by all the critics who ventured into his works, for some of them, though always recognizing the highly poetic nature of his texts, often accused him of artificiality, based on arguments such as the one that the type of language used by his characters is inappropriate to their cultural level. Although these arguments cannot be totally dismissed – there is no doubt that Rosa's use of language is peculiar and does not correspond to any empirical reality – we cannot fail to observe that the artificiality these critics point out, far from being, as they implied, something that stands in opposi-

---

[37] Eduardo Portella, "Um romance síntese," *Correio da Manhã* [Rio de Janeiro], 1 December 1956, 1º Cad., p. 10. This article will hereafter be cited as "RS."

tion to realism, is rather an aspect which contributes to it, in the sense that it brings about, by eliminating any sort of illusionism, a more authentic representation of reality. The artificiality of Rosa's narratives is aesthetic artificiality, that is, the result of his consciousness of the aesthetic nature of his works, and since realism in art is a question of inner coherence rather than of faithfulness to the outside world, there is no point in criticizing his language based on criteria of correspondence to the real spoken language in that world. The characters of Guimarães Rosa are ideal creations, not copies of real life; thus the type of language they speak could not by any means be restricted to the reproduction of a material reality.

The fact that Guimarães Rosa's characters express themselves in a kind of language that does not faithfully correspond to any palpable reality, far from constituting a weakness on the author's part, is therefore an aspect which reveals the great knowledge he has of his material. Before proceeding with our discussion of the use of this type of language, let us add here that such an aspect also had an important consequence that marks a step forward in the evolution of Latin American fiction, a step which consists of the elimination of the contrast previously existing in the work of the regionalist novelists between the narrative and descriptive passages and the dialogues of the characters. Whereas in that kind of fiction the narrative and descriptive passages were reported in an erudite kind of language which indicated the cultural status of the author, and the dialogues were constructed in a colloquial or regionalist language that conferred upon them the character of a purely folkloric object, in Rosa's narratives this distinction disappears, giving way very often to a sole and continuous discourse that, in the case of *Grande ertão: veredas,* has been designated by Galvão as "um grande unificador estilístico" (*As formas do falso,* p. 70).

However, if it is true that the type of language employed by Guimarães Rosa in his works is above all an aesthetic creation, it is also fundamental to remember that, here again, the author never dissociates it completely from the material reality which served as point of departure, namely the dialect spoken in the region which forms the setting for his stories. On the contrary, the type of language used by Rosa is crammed with terms and constructions characteristic of the sertão, and is marked by a rhythm and a certain cadence, a highly emotional content and a special way of saying things not usually found in any other area where Portuguese is spoken. Although it is not our purpose to enumerate these elements here – this task has already been performed by the critics who wrote specific studies about the linguistic or philological aspects of Rosa's works (see note 18) – it is worth mentioning that this "regionalist" component constitutes a significant portion of the author's language, and that it forms what we can designate here as the "realistic" side of his style, that is, the documental aspect which derived from his own experience in the backlands and from his observation of the linguistic habits of the backlands man.

The mixture of these aspects, characteristic of the backlands oral language, with a highly erudite component, typical of literary language, confers upon Rosa's style its "synthesis" character, responsible for the neutralization of the opposition between realism and imagination. But if the simple existence of this "synthesis" character constitutes reasonable evidence for the occurrence of such a neutralization, this fact becomes even more evident when we see that the elements which form this synthesis are not always easily identifiable as belonging to one or the other category, but rather often confusable, to the point of having led several critics to commit serious mistakes in their attempts to classify them in their studies.

An example of these elements is a series of terms and constructions which, though having disappeared in the contemporary Portuguese spoken both in Europe and in the developed areas of Brazil, are still commonly employed in some regions of the backlands which, owing to the precariousness of the means of communication, have remained immune to the progress of modern civilization. These forms, considered archaic by some of Rosa's critics, were revealed by Proença as also being regionalisms, and the critic expresses his difficulty in classifying them when he states: "Assinalar arcaísmos é tarefa... delicada, de vez que muitos regionalismos brasileiros são formas arcaicas ainda vigentes, sendo assim arriscado estabelecer até onde houve aproveitamento da linguagem dialetal ou empréstimo da língua antiga" (*Trilhas*, p. 73).

Although the example just given may be enough to indicate the difficulty of tracing a neat barrier in Rosa's style between the elements characteristic of the backlands oral language and those which are typical of literary language, this difficulty is not exclusively related to the level of words but applies also to the use of some procedures which, though seeming at first to be characteristic of literary language, actually constitute a common trait in the speech of the backlands man. The most important of these procedures – to mention just one more example – owing to the frequency with which it is employed in Rosa's texts, consists of the use of neologisms, often pointed out by critics as a highly erudite aspect of his style; yet Rosa himself defined it in *Tutaméia* as a feature widely exploited by the inhabitants of the sertão. In this book – the last one published during his lifetime – which constitutes a kind of ars poetica in the sense that he discusses some of the basic aspects of his aesthetic theory, the author, after defending the right to create words and citing several distinguished writers who adopted this practice, affirms that neologisms are commonly found in the language spoken in the sertão and concludes: "Nascem, ninguém sabe como; vivem eternamente ou desaparecem um dia sem também se saber como."[38] For Rosa, people from the sertão, unlike average educated people, have a simple and limited vocabulary, and since their view of the world is predominantly intuitive they find the creation of words imperative, be it, as he explains, "por rigor de mostrar a vivo a vida," or "por gosto ou capricho de transmitirem com obscuridade coerente suas próprias e obscuras intuições" (*Tutaméia*, p. 66). These people are, he continues, in this sense very close to the poet; thus we may conclude that when Rosa makes use of this procedure in his works he is not exclusively revealing an erudite or sophisticated consciousness but is also expressing the spirit of the backlands man, or rather the popular life-trend this man carries in his veins.

4.6. *Guimarães Rosa's Aesthetic Revolution*

4.6.1. *Revitalization and Commitment*

Now that we have defined the "synthesis" character of Rosa's style and discussed the neutralization of the opposition between realism and fantasy on the level of language stricto sensu, an

---

[38] João Guimarães Rosa, *Tutaméia* (Rio de Janeiro: José Olympio, 1967), p. 66.

observation becomes necessary: the fact that such a neutralization is also effected on this level constitutes one more piece of evidence of the integration existing in *Grande sertão: veredas* between form and content and consequently contributes to confer upon the novel the character of totality which Harss considered in *Into the Mainstream* as one of the most distinguishing features of the "new narrative" of Latin America. It was the recognition of this integration that led a critic like Augusto de Campos to affirm in his essay "Um lance de 'dês' do *Grande sertão*" that "os grandes conteúdos de *Grande sertão*, como os de Joyce, se resolvem não só *através da*, mas *na* linguagem" (p. 41), and to apply to Rosa's book a statement similar to that which the critic Harry Levin once used in relation to *Finnegans Wake:* that the real novel is the one that takes place between the author and his language.[39]

Although the observation regarding the integration in *Grande sertão: veredas* between the author's world view and the means to express it was made earlier when we discussed the structural levels of the narrative, and showed how the protagonist's existential quest is accomplished through the search for a new type of language, our insistence upon the issue becomes an indispensable matter at this point because this aspect of the novel indicates, better perhaps than any other, that "a invenção para Rosa," as Eduardo Portella affirms, "não é um devaneio formal,"[40] and constitutes a response to the accusation, made by a few conservative critics, that Rosa indulged in innovatory undertakings for their own sake and had consequently fallen into the field of pure ludism. If the word for Rosa is not a mere vehicle for the transmission of ideas but rather something which, as Portella states, derives "da dinâmica do pensar" ("RS," p. x), or in other words if it is a *logos* and not a *verbum*, as another critic once affirmed, using Heraclitus's distinction,[41] then the innovations the author introduces into his texts can by no means be gratuitous, a mere play-with-words. They are, on the contrary, the very expression of the author's world wiew and therefore play a fundamental role in the narrative.

---

[39] Harry Levin, *James Joyce, A critical Introduction* (Norfolk, Conn.: New Directions, 1941), p. 194.

[40] Eduardo Portella, "A estória cont(r)a a história," *Jornal do Brasil* [Rio de Janeiro], 30 December 1967, Cad. B, p. 3.

[41] Afonso Arinos de Melo Franco, "O verbo e o logos," in *Em memória de João Guimarães Rosa* (Rio de Janeiro: José Olympio, 1968), pp. 89-106.

The fact that Guimarães Rosa's linguistic innovations are not a mere play-with-words was recognized, for example, by Augusto de Campos, who, after affirming that in *Grande sertão: veredas* "as mais ousadas invenções lingüísticas estão sempre em relação isomórfica com o conteúdo" ("Um lance de 'dês',"p. 56), reached the point of demonstrating how even the insistent use of certain phonemes, such as /d/ and /n/, in key passages of the novel was not done at random, for they also serve a special semantic function, and therefore play an important role in the narrative. The phoneme /d/, the critic affirms, has its semantic correlate in the protagonist's existential conflict between good and evil, which is represented in the novel by the dichotomy "Deus ou o Demo" ("God or the Devil"), constituted by two words of an equal number of letters and sounds, both starting with a /d/. This phoneme, he continues, is alliterated in the text every time the protagonist's existential conflict is closely focused upon and is also significantly present in the name of Diadorim, a figure that, as we have seen, constitutes the embodiment of that conflict. This character's name is, in his words, "um caleidoscópio em miniatura de reverberações semânticas, suscitadas por associação formal" (ibid.,p. 60), and as such it contains in its own form the nucleus of the conflict mentioned, which he explains by dividing the name into two lines:

a) Dia + adora
                    + im
b) Diá + dor

Whereas the first line (a), composed of the noun *dia* 'day' and the verb form *adora* (from *adorar* 'to adore'), indicates all the positive aspects of Diadorim's influence upon Riobaldo, the second line (b), composed of the nouns *diá* (short for *diabo* 'devil,' frequently used in certain regions of Brazil) and *dor* 'pain,' expresses the negative aspects of that influence; and, finally, the reduced form *-im* of the diminutive suffix *-inho, -inha*, applicable in Portugues to both a male and a female name, complements the character's ambiguity by clearly suggesting his androgynous status.

The phoneme /n/, according to Campos, just like the /d/, also plays a significant role in the text of *Grande sertão: veredas*, and it is usually associated with the theme of negation, of the absurdity of life, represented by the figure of the devil. It is with this connotation that it is so abundantly used in the passages which mark Riobaldo's unsuccessful attempts to find and assume his own identity and is also often present in the various names with which the devil is designated in the book: *o-que-não fala, o-que-não-ri, o-que-nunca-se-ri, o-que-não-existe*, etc. However, since for Rosa the state of not-being is frequently related to that of being in the sense that it contains the germs of a potential essence – let us not forget that in *Grande sertão: veredas* "Tudo é e não é" (13) – the phoneme is also frequently alliterated to indicate this potential essence, thus leading to a neutralization not only of the opposition between being and not-being, but also of every kind of world view based on radical dichotomies. It is in this latter sense that it is so insistently employed, for instance in the following passage, found in the episode of the siege at the Tucanos farm, which marks a decisive step in Riobaldo's process of assuming his own identity: "–Pois é, Chefe. E eu sou nada, não sou nada, não sou nada... Não sou mesmo nada, nadinha de nada, de nada... Sou a coisinha nenhuma, o senhor sabe? Sou o nada coisinha mesma nenhuma de nada, o menorzinho de todos. O senhor sabe? De nada. De nada... De nada..." (331). In this speech, the protagonist, by using a series of negatives which indicate on the denotative level his impotence before the presence of his leader, is on the contrary affirming his own power and making known his capacity for facing the latter and assuming the command of his group.

Augusto de Campos's statement, discussed in detail in the essay just cited and exemplified above, to the effect that every formal element employed by Guimarães Rosa in *Grande sertão: veredas* is always in an isomorphic relationship with the content of the narrative certainly constitutes a support for our affirmation that the author's linguistic innovations, far from being gratuitous, play a significant role in the narrative. However, since Campos, owing to the very nature and purpose of his study, does not enter into considerations about the function of these innovations as a whole, we will continue with a reference to another critic, Franklin de Oliveira, who in "Guimarães Rosa" went a little farther than Campos in this matter, asserting that Rosa's stylistic revolution is not something isolated but instead a part of a wider revolution in the sense that it "reveste-se, também, do sentido de protesto contra a sociedade tecnológica," which is, according to him, "a civilização que gerou a antilinguagem." For Oliveira, this one-dimensional kind of civilization had reduced language to a mere series of clichés and stereotyped formulae, and Guimarães Rosa, by abandoning this type of language and restoring what the critic calls the "imprevisibilidade criativa da forma literária," was not only expressing his refusal of a sterile sort of language but also raising a full protest against the kind of society of which such a language is a typical manifestation, and consequently offering a critical view of reality, which is, as we know, at the basis of every truly revolutionary kind of literature ("Guimarães Rosa," p. 443).

This observation made by Oliveira about Rosa's linguistic innovations is of primary relevance because, by asserting that the criticism of language implies that of society, the critic calls attention to two fundamental aspects that had escaped the majority of his colleagues – the relationship existing in the novel between language and society, and the critical character which language assumes in the text – and consequently indicates, though in an indirect manner, the scope of those innovations. Although the two aspects mentioned are intimately connected – the element of criticism is the common denominator – we will discuss them separately, to see in what way they contribute to confer upon the author's innovations a dimension which transcends their purely aesthetic purposes. However, it is first worth observing that whereas the first of these aspects is of a more direct nature, in that it simply refers to the relationship between the two terms, the second, of a wider scope, throws clearer light upon the subject and therefore illustrates, in a more thorough manner, the point we are trying to make.

As far as the first aspect is concerned, we will simply recall our affirmation that for Guimarães Rosa the language of a people is intimately connected with the people's way of thinking, with its own view of the world, and add that if it is true, as the author seems firmly to believe, that in order to offer a new view of the world it is necessary to begin by changing the language which reflects it, the alteration of this language in turn may generate a different world view. As the critic Bernardo Gersen appropriately remarks in an article on Rosa entitled "Veredas no *Grande sertão*," "a recriação da linguagem produz uma visão, não-habitual do mundo, através da qual objetos, paisagens e criaturas assumem novos contornos, surgem libertos das formas tradicionais decorrentes de nossas padronizadas representações subjetivas."[42] Man's vision of objects, he continues, is linked to his habits and his verbal associations, and the conventional expression and the order of words in the sentence, for example, which reflect the disposition of objects and the order of the surrounding world, were determined on a large scale by his practical experience in time and space. Thus, if an author disrupts the habitual organization of words and alters the syntactic structure of the sentences, he may cause a transformation in the world perceived through them: the contour of the objects and their relationship, the attitudes and gestures of the persons who pronounce the words usually associated with a certain way of speaking, may change.

However, if the aspect just discussed indicates the importance of Rosa's linguistic innovations by suggesting, though in an indirect way, the role they may have in the creation of a new world view, the total scope of his stylistic revolution will be made clear only after we discuss the second aspect mentioned – what we have called the critical character of language or, rather, its character as an instrument of action and human fulfillment. For Guimarães Rosa, language is a powerful instrument of action in the sense that, by expressing ideas – "el idioma sirve para expresar ideas," he says in his interview with Lorenz ("Diálogo," p. 42) – it may act upon people's minds by illuminating their consciousness. But as this power of language is weakened or even lost whenever its forms are worn out and conditioned to a specific world view, it becomes necessary to renew these forms in order to restore such a power. And since it is only by so doing that language may recover its capacity to illuminate people's consciousness, the act of renewing it acquires an ethical significance which Rosa himself explains when he affirms that human welfare depends, among other things, on man's very capacity to revitalize language.

It is to this ethical character present in the necessity of restoring to language its power of action that Guimarães Rosa refers when he speaks, still in that interview, of a "compromiso del corazón" which, according to him, every writer must have. For the

---

[42] Bernardo Gersen, "Veredas no *Grande sertão*," *O Estado de São Paulo*, 24 March 1962, Supl. Lit., p. 6.

author of *Grande sertão: veredas*, literature is the art of language, and the novelist's task, like that of every artist, is to reveal and unfold, not simply portray, as the Naturalist and Neo-Naturalist writers of Latin America believed it to be; and since it is not possible to perform these functions by means of a worn-out kind of language, he more than anyone else is expected to revitalize it every time its power is weakened or lost, by constantly renewing its forms. Man's current, everyday language is unfit for literature precisely because it has lost its capacity to express ideas; as Rosa states, "El lenguaje corriente expresa tan sólo rutinas y no ideas" (Lorenz, p. 42). Thus it becomes a duty for every writer who wants to accomplish his task adequately to explore the originality of linguistic expression, so that the latter may recover its power and be able to act again upon people's minds. For this reason he affirms to Lorenz that poetry (here taken as literature in general) "se origina de la modificación de realidades idiomáticas" (ibid., p. 44), and later concludes, with total conviction, that every true writer is also a revolutionary, because, by restoring language's power of action, he is certainly also contributing to the illumination of people's consciousness and spreading the seeds of possible transformations.

4.6.2. The Role of the Reader

However, if it is true that by revitalizing language's original strength the writer is fulfilling his mission as an artist of the word, and is therefore contributing to the illumination of people's consciousness, or as Harss puts it, to the awakening of man's soul (Harss & Dohmann, p. 149), the scope of Rosa's stylistic revolution does not stop at this point, for the author places an emphasis upon the reader's process of reflection and on the transformation of the world perceived by him. For Guimarães Rosa, it is not enough to illuminate the reader's consciousness, to express a series of ideas that might lead him to see beyond apparent reality, but also, and very specially, he must be induced to reflect and to search, as a consequence, for a new view of the world. Thus by disrupting the worn-out form of language and by exploring the potentialities of linguistic expression, Guimarães Rosa is not simply restoring the power of the poetic *dictum*, however fundamental this function may be, but is also making use of a device, similar to Brecht's critical distancing, to lead the reader into a whole process of questioning, and consequently to transform him from a mere passive consumer into an active participant in the reality represented.

Although this emphasis on the reader's process of reflection can be detected in every procedure employed for the revitalization of literary language – from the strictly linguistic ones up to those on the level of narrative structure – it might be worthwhile to mention here two of these procedures which, because of their importance in the narrative, are appropriate to illustrate the question: the inconclusive character of the narrative – which ends as it begins, in a kind of psychic present – marked by the symbol of infinity suggesting eternal continuity, and the questioning the narrator undertakes about his own way of telling the story, which is represented in the novel by an entire structural subline that we have designated as metalinguistic. However, since these procedures have already been commented upon in our discussion of the structural levels of the narrative, we will mention them only briefly here simply to show the importance of Rosa's transformation, by means of concrete narrative devices, of the role of the reader from a mere spectator into an active participant.

We have seen when discussing the structure of *Grande sertão: veredas* that Riobaldo's narrative is a continuous process of search developed in the presence of the reader in the very act of narration and for this reason it does not reach a terminal point by the time the novel is over but, on the contrary, is simply interrupted, leaving the path free for further speculation. Although this inconclusive character of the narrative is basically a result of the fact that it is presented as a phase in the process of growth through which the protagonist goes – let us not forget that Riobaldo had already reported the same events to his compadre Quelemém and had not seen them from the same perspective – this device strongly contributes, as we shall see now, to transforming the reader into a coparticipant in the work. Riobaldo sets out to report to his interlocutor the story of his life as a jagunço with the clear purpose of dissipating doubts that had remained in his consciousness as a result of those past experiences, and at the end of his long monologue-dialogue he attains, at least to a certain extent, some kind of comfort or relief; however, the process of search in which he is involved does not stop at this point, for the doubts that disturbed him, if or when resolved, are replaced by new ones, in a dialectical manner that has no possible end. And since at the end of this trajectory the only definite conclusion at which he may arrive is the realization that "vivendo, se aprende; mas o que se aprende, mais, é só a fazer outras maiores perguntas" (389-90), as he himself says at a certain point along his way, the reader is also involved in this ongoing process and is driven, by means of meditating upon the facts narrated, to continue the search initiated by the narrator. Thus the search for self-knowledge accomplished by the protagonist is extended to the reader, who incorporates it into his own living experience and becomes, in turn, another narrator, giving origin to a kind of chain which would gradually increase its length every time a new person takes on the task of reading the novel. For this reason the interlocutor is presented in the narrative as a double figure; on the one hand he is the one who listens to the story – that is, a representative of the reader; on the other he also is an image of the writer, who, having taken notes while listening, will transmit the story to others in the form of a book.

But if the inconclusive character of the narrative may not be totally satisfactory to evidence the transformation of the traditional type of reader into a coparticipant in the work, the other procedure mentioned – the narrator's questioning of his own way of telling the story – leaves no more doubts on the subject. When the narrator of *Grande sertão: veredas* interrupts his report to comment upon his own technique, he is calling upon the reader to reflect not only about the facts narrated but also about the very way of transmitting them through language, and is attributing to him a weight of responsibility which he could not otherwise have, for he is being urged to become both a critic and a collaborator in the work. The narrator is aware of the relative character of his own view of reality; thus, rather than offering his reader the product of his reflections, he presents to him these reflections in the very act of their being made. And as they are submitted to a constant process of questioning, the reader is driven not only to take a position about them but also to search, in turn, for his own view of the world. Therefore, rather than being a passive consumer of the work, the receiver of a ready-made world view in whose formation he cannot participate, he is transformed into an agent, a possible modifier of the reality represented. And since such a reality, represented in the work of art, is in a dialectical relationship with the outside world, this active role of the reader is extended beyond the book's pages.

This stimulation of the process of reflection on the part of the reader and his consequent transformation from a mere passive consumer into an active participant in the work constitutes the ultimate function of Rosa's stylistic revolution – its active function, if we may call it so – and this very element confers upon such a revolution a status which transcends its strictly aesthetic purposes. There is no doubt that Rosa's revolution is essentially an aesthetic one in the sense that it is both accomplished within literature and aimed at the innovation of the means of literary production, but the fact that it places the reader at the core of the process makes it cross the barriers of literature and project itself into a sphere of concrete human action. Guimarães Rosa is aware of the fact, as he states through the words of Riobaldo, that "toda ação principia mesmo é por uma palavra pensada. Palavra pegante, dada ou guardada, que vai rompendo rumo" (170); thus he provides his reader, by means of the revolution he effects, with this "palavra pensada"; and by constantly stimulating the reader's reflection upon and participation in it, induces him to question also his own reality and to search, as a consequence, for his own way of acting upon it. In this sense he constructs a novel which is, even in sociopolitical terms, of a more "committed" kind than those of the so-called writers of the revolution because, whereas the latter limited themselves to talking about the necessity of a revolution and did not go beyond offering their readers a series of ready-made ideas which maintained their position of passive consumers, the author of *Grande sertão: veredas* makes this revolution real within the strict field of literature, and by revealing his technique he reaches the reader in a much more effective manner.

It is true that Rosa's stylistic revolution, if taken by itself, cannot be totally responsible for conferring upon his novel a "committed" character, at least in the traditional sense of the term, for the social preoccupation which constituted the center of attention in the "novel of the revolution" that immediately preceded Rosa's and the works of the other "new novelists" of Latin America continues to be an essential element in *Grande sertão: veredas*, as we have seen, for example, when discussing the issues of the jagunço and the sertão and the opposition between objective realism and other levels of reality. Furthermore, the importance of these social elements in the corpus of *Grande sertão: veredas* has already been demonstrated by critics who approached the novel from a sociological perspective. However, what is important to stress here is that it is owing to the revolution accomplished on the level of language and narrative structure that these very elements become effective, in sociopolitical as well as artistic terms, because the author reaches the reader in a much more thoroughgoing manner. Here we come to a point, crucial for the understanding of *Grande sertão: veredas:* it is by means of the author's aesthetic, or rather aestheticist, preoccupations that he builds up a novel, of a profound critical nature, which can also be placed side by side with the paradigms of great "realist" art.

Contrary to the practice of the writers of the "novel of the revolution," who professed that literature should offer a faithful picture of outside reality for the purpose of awakening man's consciousness toward the social, political, or economic problems which afflicted him, Guimarães Rosa believed as Portella affirms in "A estória cont(r)a a história," that "somente estando contra a história, a estória conta a história" (p. 3), and he creates a work of a self-conscious kind, which constantly questions its own status as fiction. However, by so doing he is more successful than those writers even in that aspect which constituted the main goal of their works, because, as another critic very accurately remarks, "quanto mais ele 'desrealiza' a realidade, mais próximo está do mistério da arte que, por extensão, é o próprio mistério da vida."[43]

Although this observation may seem an absurd paradox, it expresses quite clearly Rosa's conception of a work of art and of the dialectical relationship it maintains with the outside world, and above all confirms the statement made at the beginning of this chapter that the author's aestheticist preoccupations, far from being in opposition to the question of social commitment, are rather very much integrated with it, for it is by moving deeply within the sphere of one of these elements that he attains the other in a more nearly complete manner. Thus at this point we may conclude by affirming that in the same way that the protagonist of *Grande sertão:*

---

[43] Francisco de Assis Brasil, *Guimarães Rosa* (Rio de Janeiro: Organizações Simões, 1969), p. 103.

veredas attains the unity and significance of his experience only by means of the search he effects for his own way of narrating those experiences, the author of the novel undertakes a similar quest for artistic perfection and, by so doing, he "alça," as Oliveira observes, "a crítica da vida feita pela arte à condição de poder revolucionário sem precedentes" ("Guimarães Rosa," p. 446).

It is this neutralization of the opposition between aestheticism and social commitment accomplished by Guimarães Rosa in *Grande sertão: veredas* that distinguishes his novel both from the traditionally called "committed" manifestations of the genre and from the pure verbal experiments, and confers upon it a stature comparable only to that of the other "new novels" of Latin America. In Rosa's novel the elements which characterize both these opposing tendencies are not only efficiently present but also entirely fused into a kind of perfect synthesis that can be defined only as critical in the widest sense of the term.

We have said with reference to the substantial critical studies that have focused on *Grande sertão: veredas* from a perspective which transcends the pure level of linguistic exegesis that all of them are in common accord as to the fact that the novel's structure is composed of a series of antagonic pairs whose opposition gradually disappears to give way to a synthesis, indicated in the text itself by the leitmotif *Tudo é e não é,* repeated therein a great number of times. In this study, however, we have seen that the synthesis mentioned in those critical works as characteristic of *Grande sertão: veredas* is not limited exclusively to the novel's component elements. Rather, this synthesis is also responsible for the neutralization of a series of oppositions which represented various traditional trends of both Brazilian and Latin American fiction as a whole, revealing, therefore, the inapplicability today of such labels as "regionalist" or "committed" imposed by the historians of literature upon the art work. We will conclude by stressing that *Grande sertão: veredas* is indeed a synthesis novel in the full sense of the term, for it not only makes use of the narrative achievements of all times, but also reconciles, as Luis Hars states, all these experiences in its own corpus. It is something like Riobaldo's religious precepts, which he defines as: "Muita religião, seu moço! Eu cá, não perco ocasião de religião. Aproveito de todas. Bebo água de todo rio" (17).

BIBLIOGRAPHY

GENERAL WORKS

Alter, Robert. *Partial Magic: The Novel as a Self-Conscious Genre.* Berkeley: Univ. of California Press, 1975.
Arvon, Henri. *Marxist Aesthetics.* Trans. Helen R. Lane. Ithaca, N.Y.: Cornell Univ. Press, 1973.
Auerbach, Erich. *Mimesis: The Representation of Reality in Western Literature.* Trans. Willard R. Trask. 1953; rpt. Princeton: Princeton Univ. Press, 1973.
Auzias, Jean Marie, et al. *Structuralisme et marxisme.* Paris: Union Générale d'Editions, 1970.
Bachelard, Gaston. *La poétique de l'espace.* 4th ed. Paris: Presses Universitaires de France, 1964.
Bakhtin, Mikhail. *Marxismo e filosofia da linguagem.* Trans. Michel Lahud and Yara Frateschi Vieira. São Paulo: Hucited, 1979.
———. *La poétique de Dostoievski.* Trans. Isabelle Kolitcheff. Paris: Seuil, 1970.
Baquero Goyanes, Mariano. *Estructuras de la novela actual.* 3rd ed. Barcelona: Editorial Planeta, 1975.
Barthes, Roland. *Critique et vérité.* Paris: Seuil, 1966.
———. *Le degré zéro de l'écriture.* Paris: Seuil, 1953.
———. *Essais critiques.* Paris: Seuil, 1964.
———. *Mythologies.* Paris: Seuil, 1957.
———. *Le plaisir du texte.* Paris: Seuil 1973.
———. *S/Z: Essais.* Paris: Seuil, 1970.
Baxandall, Lee, and Stefan Morawski, eds. *Marx and Engels on Literature and Art: A Selection of Writings.* St. Louis, Mo.: Telos Press, 1973.
Benjamin, Walter. *Illuminations.* Trans. Harry Zohn. New York: Harcourt, Brace & World, 1968.
Bergonzi, Bernard. *The Situation of the Novel.* Critical Essays in Modern Literature Series. 2nd ed. Pittsburgh: Univ. of Pittsburgh Press, 1972.
Bessière, Irène. *Le récit fantastique: la poétique de l'incertain.* Paris: Librairie Larousse, 1974.
Booth, Wayne C. *The Rhetoric of Fiction.* 10th ed. Chicago: Univ. of Chicago Press, 1973.
Bradbury, Malcom, and James McFarlane, eds. *Modernism 1890-1930.* 2nd ed. Harmondsworth, Eng.: Penguin Books, 1978.
Bremond, Claude. *Logique du récit.* Paris: Seuil, 1973.

Brooks, Cleanth, and Robert Penn Warren, eds. *Understanding Fiction.* 2nd ed. New York: Appleton-Century-Crofts, 1959.

Burns, Emile, ed. *The Marxist Reader: The Most Significant and Enduring Works of Marxism.* New York: Avenel Books, 1982.

Coelho, Eduardo Prado, ed. *Estruturalismo: antologia de textos teóricos.* Porto: Portugália Editora, 1968.

Communications. Publications de l'Ecole Pratique des Hautes Etudes, No. 8 (1966), No. 11 (1968). Paris: Seuil, 1966, 1968.

Connolly, Cyril. *The Modern Movement: 100 Key Books from England, France and America, 1880-1950.* London: Deutsch, 1965.

Coseriu, Eugenio. *Sistema, norma y habla.* Montevideo: Universidad de la República, 1952.

Coutinho, Afrânio. *Da crítica e da nova crítica.* 2nd ed. Rio de Janeiro: Civilização Brasileira, 1975.

Culler, Jonathan. *Structuralist Poetics: Structuralism, Linguistics and the Study of Literature.* 2nd ed. Ithaca, N.Y.: Cornell Univ. Press, 1976.

Daiches, David. *Critical Approaches to Literature.* Englewood Cliffs, N.J.: Prentice-Hall, 1956.

Demetz, Peter. *Marx, Engels and the Poets: Origins of Marxist Literary Criticism.* Trans. Jeffrey Sammons. Chicago: Univ. of Chicago Press, 1967.

Derrida, Jacques. *L'écriture et la différence.* Paris: Seuil, 1967.

Doubrovsky, Serge. *Pourquoi la nouvelle critique: critique et objectivité.* Paris: Mercure de France, 1966.

Eagleton, Terry. *Marxism and Literary Criticism.* Berkeley: Univ. of California Press, 1976.

Eco, Umberto. *Apocalittici e integrati.* Milan: Bompiani, 1965.

———. *Opera aperta.* Milan: Bompiani, 1962.

Ehrmann, Jacques, ed. *Structuralism.* Garden City, N.J.: Doubleday, 1970.

Ellis, John M. *The Theory of Literary Criticism: A Logical Analysis.* Berkeley: Univ. of California Press, 1974.

Ellman, Richard, and Charles Fidelson, eds. *The Modern Tradition: Backgrounds of Modern Literature.* New York: Oxford Univ. Press, 1965.

Erlich, Victor. *Russian Formalism: History-Doctrine.* The Hague: Mouton, 1955.

Falk, Eugene. *Types of Thematic Structure: The Nature and Function of Motifs in Gide, Camus, and Sartre.* 2nd ed. Chicago: Univ. of Chicago Press, 1972.

Faulkner, Peter. *Modernism: The Critical Idiom.* London: Methuen, 1977.

Fehér, Ferenc. *O romance está morrendo?* Trans. Eduardo Lima. Rio de Janeiro: Paz e Terra, 1972.

Fischer, Ernst. *The Necessity of Art: A Marxist Approach.* Trans. Anna Bostock. Harmondsworth, Eng.: Penguin Books, 1963.

Forster, E. M. *Aspects of the Novel.* 2nd ed. London: Edward Arnold, 1928.

Foucault, Michel. *Les mots et les choses.* Paris: Gallimard, 1966.

Frank, Joseph. "Spatial Form in Modern Literature." In *The Widening Gyre: Crisis and Mastery in Modern Literature.* New Brunswick, N. J.: Rutges Univ. Press, 1963, pp. 3-62.

Freedman, Ralph. *The Lyrical Novel. Studies in H. Hesse, A. Gide and V. Woolf.* Princeton: Princeton Univ. Press, 1966.

Friedman, Alan. *The Turn of the Novel.* New York: Oxford Univ. Press, 1966.

Friedman, Norman. *Form and Meaning in Fiction.* Athens: Univ. of Georgia Press, 1975.

Frye, Northrop. *The Anatomy of Criticism: Four Essays.* Princeton: Princeton Univ. Press, 1957.

Frye, Northrop. *The Critical Path: An Essay on the Social Context of Literary Criticism.* Bloomington: Indiana Univ. Press, 1971.
———. *The Stubborn Structure: Essays on Criticism and Society.* Ithaca, N.Y.: Cornell Univ. Press, 1970.
Geismar, Maxwell. *American Moderns: From Rebellion to Conformity.* New York: Hill and Wang, 1958.
Genette, Gérard. *Figures: Essais.* Paris: Seuil, 1966.
———. *Figures II: Essais.* Paris: Seuil, 1969.
———. *Figures III.* Paris: Seuil, 1972.
Goldknopf, David. *The Life of the Novel.* Chicago: Univ. of Chicago Press, 1972.
Goldman, Lucien. *Pour une sociologie du roman.* Paris: Gallimard, 1964.
Gras, Vernon W., ed. *European Literary Theory and Practice: From Existential Phenomenology to Structuralism.* New York: Dell, 1973.
Guerard, Albert J. *The Triumph of the Novel: Dickens, Dostoievsky, Faulkner.* New York: Oxford Univ. Press, 1976.
Hartman, Geoffrey H. *Beyond Formalism: Literary Essays 1958-70.* New Haven: Yale Univ. Press, 1970.
Hauser, Arnold. *The Social History of Art.* Trans. Stanley Godman. 2 vols. London: Routledge and Kegan Paul, 1951.
Hemmings, F. W. J., ed. *The Age of Realism.* Harmondsworth, Eng.: Penguin Books, 1974.
Hodin, J. P. *The Dilemma of Being Modern: Essays on Art and Literature.* London: Routledge and Kegan Paul, 1956.
Howe, Irving, ed. *The Idea of the Modern in Literature and the Arts.* New York: Horizon Press, 1967.
———. *Politics and the Novel: The Classic Study of the Impact of Ideology on Literature.* Chicago: Discus Books, 1970.
Humphrey, Robert. *Stream of Consciousness in the Modern Novel.* 1954; rpt. Berkeley: Univ. of California Press, 1972.
Ingarden, Roman. *The Cognition of the Literary Work of Art.* Trans. Ruth A. Crowley and Kenneth R. Olson. Evanston: Northwestern Univ. Press, 1973.
Jakobson, Roman. *Essais de linguistique générale.* Paris: Ed. de Minuit, 1963.
James, Henry. *The Art of the Novel: Critical Prefaces.* New York: Scribner's Sons, 1941.
Jameson, Fredric. *Marxism and Form: Twentieth-Century Dialectical Theories of Literature.* 1972; rpt. Princeton: Princeton Univ. Press, 1974.
———. *The Prison-House of Language: A Critical Account of Structuralism and Russian Formalism.* Princeton: Princeton Univ. Press, 1974.
Kahler, Erich. *The Inward Turn of Narrative.* Trans. Richard and Clara Winston. Princeton: Princeton Univ. Press, 1973.
Kampf, Louis. *On Modernism: The Prospects for Literature and Freedom.* Cambridge: MIT Press, 1967.
Kayser, Wolfgang. *Fundamentos da interpretação e da análise literária.* 2 vols. Coimbra: Armênio Amado Editor, 1948.
Kazin. Alfred. *On Native Grounds: An Interpretation of Modern American Prose Literature.* New York: Harcourt Brace Jovanovich, 1970.
Kenner, Hugh. *The Pound Era.* Berkeley: Univ. of California Press, 1971.
Kermode, Frank. *The Sense of an Ending: Studies in the Theory of Fiction.* New York: Oxford Univ. Press, 1967.
Kristeva, Julia. *La révolution du langage poétique.* Paris: Seuil, 1974.
Lane, Michael, ed. *Structuralism: A Reader.* London: Jonathan Cape, 1970.
Langbaum, Robert. *The Modern Spirit: Essays on the Continuity of Nineteenth- and Twentieth-Century Literature.* New York: Oxford Univ. Press, 1970.

Leavis, F. R. *The Great Tradition: George Eliot, Henry James, Joseph Conrad.* London: Chatto and Windus, 1948.
Levin, Harry. *The Gates of Horn.* New York: Oxford Univ. Press, 1963.
———. *James Joyce, a Critical Introduction.* Norfolk, Conn.: New Directions, 1941.
Lima, Luís Costa, ed. *Teoria da literatura em suas fontes.* Rio de Janeiro: Livraria Francisco Alves Editora, 1975.
Lubbock, Percy. *The Craft of Fiction.* 1921; rpt. New York: Viking Press, 1973.
Lukács, Georg. *Realism in Our Time. Literature and the Class Struggle.* Trans. John Mander and Necke Mander. New York: Harper and Row, 1971.
———. *La Signification présente du Réalisme critique.* Trans. Maurice T. Gandillac. Paris: Gallimard, 1960.
———. *The Theory of the Novel.* Trans. Anna Bostock. Cambridge: MIT Press, 1968.
McElroy, Davis Dunbar. *Existentialism and Modern Literature.* New York: Citadel Press, 1963.
Meyerhoff, Hans. *Time in Literature.* Berkeley: Univ. of California Press, 1968.
Narrative and Narratives. New Literary History: A Journal of Theory and Interpretation, 6, No. 2 (Winter 1975).
Narratologie. Poétique: revue de théorie et d'analyse littéraires, 6, No. 24 (1975).
Ortega y Gasset, J. "La deshumanización del arte e ideas sobre la novela." In *Obras.* Madrid: Espasa-Calpe, 1932, pp. 887-958.
Poétique: revue de théorie et d'analyse littéraires, No. 53 (Feb. 1983) – Ecriture et altérité.
Portella, Eduardo. *Fundamento da investigação literária.* Rio de Janeiro: Tempo Brasileiro, 1974.
Read, Herbert. *English Prose Style.* London: G. Bell and Sons, 1956.
Scholes, Robert, ed. *Approaches to the Novel: Materials for a Poetics.* Rev. ed. San Francisco: Chandler, 1966.
Scholes, Robert, and Robert Kellogg. *The Nature of Narrative.* New York: Oxford Univ. Press, 1966.
Segre, Cesare. *Semiotics and Literary Criticism.* Trans. John Meddemmen. The Hague: Mouton, 1973.
Silva, Vítor Manuel de Aguiar e. *Teoria da literatura.* São Paulo: Livraria Martins Fontes Ed., 1976.
Spears, Monroe K. *Dionysus and the City: Modernism in Twentieth-Century Poetry.* New York: Oxford Univ. Press, 1970.
Spencer, Sharon. *Space, Time and Structure in the Modern Novel.* Chicago: Swallow Press, 1971.
Spender, Stephen. *The Struggle of the Modern.* London: Hamish Hamilton, 1963.
Spilka, Mark, ed. *Towards a Poetics of Fiction.* Bloomington: Indiana Univ. Press, 1977.
Spitzer, Leo. *Linguistics and Literary History.* Princeton: Princeton Univ. Press, 1948.
Strelka, J., ed. *Problems of Literary Evaluation.* University Park: Pennsylvania State Univ. Press, 1969.
Todorov, Tzvetan. *As estruturas narrativas.* Trans. Leila Perrone-Moisés. São Paulo: Perspectiva, 1969.
———. *Introduction à la littérature fantastique.* Paris: Seuil, 1970.
———. *Littérature et signification.* Paris: Larousse, 1967.
———. *Poétique de la prose.* Paris: Seuil, 1971.
———, ed. *Théorie de la littérature: Textes des formalistes russes.* Paris: Seuil, 1966.
Torre, Guillermo de. *Historia de las literaturas de vanguardia.* Madrid: Ediciones Guadarrama, 1965.

Trilling, Lionel. *The Liberal Imagination*. New York: Viking Press, 1950.
Trotsky, Leon. *Literature and Revolution*. Trans. Rose Trimsky. Ann Arbor: Univ. of Michigan Press, 1960, Paperback Ed.
Watt, Ian. *The Rise of the Novel: Studies in Defoe, Richardson, and Fielding*. Berkeley: Univ. of California Press, 1957.
Wellek, René. *Concepts of Criticism*. New Haven: Yale Univ. Press, 1963.
———, and Austin Warren. *Theory of Literature*. New York: Harcourt, Brace, 1949.
Wilson, Edmund. *Axel's Castle: A Study in the Imaginative Literature of 1870-1930*. 1931; rpt. New York: Scribner's Sons, 1969.
———. *The Triple Thinkers: Twelve Essays on Literary Subjects*. 1948; rpt. New York: Farrar, Straus and Giroux, 1976.

WORKS ON LATIN AMERICAN LITERATURE

BOOKS

Aínsa, Fernando. *Identidad cultural de Iberoamérica en su narrativa*. Madrid: Gredos, 1986.
Alegría, Fernando. *Historia de la novela hispanoamericana*. 3rd ed. Mexico: Ed. de Andrea, 1966.
———. *Literatura y revolución*. Mexico: Fondo de Cultura Económica, 1971.
Amorós, Andrés. *Introducción a la novela hispanoamericana actual*. Salamanca: Anaya, 1973.
Anderson-Imbert, Enrique. *Crítica interna*. Madrid: Taurus, 1960.
———. *Literatura hispanoamericana*. 2 vols. Mexico: Fondo de Cultura Económica, 1961.
Avalle-Arce, J. B. *Narradores hispanoamericanos de hoy*. Chapel Hill: Univ. of North Carolina Press, 1973.
Bellini, Giuseppe. *Il laberinto mágico: Studi sul "nuovo romanzo" ispano-americano*. Milan: Cisalpino-Goliardica, 1973.
Benedetti, Mario. *Letras del continente mestizo*. Montevideo: Ed. Arca, 1967.
Bleznick, Donald W., ed. *Variaciones interpretativas en torno a la nueva narrativa hispanoamericana*. Santiago de Chile: Helmy F. Giacoman, 1972.
Bosi, Alfredo. *História concisa da literatura brasileira*. São Paulo: Cultrix, 1970.
Brasil, Francisco de Assis. *A nova literatura*. Vol. I. Rio de Janeiro: Cia. Ed. Americana, 1973.
Brotherston, Gordon. *The Emergence of the Latin American Novel*. Cambridge: Cambridge Univ. Press, 1977.
Brushwood, John L. *The Spanish-American Novel: A XXth Century Survey*. Austin: Univ. of Texas Press, 1975.
Cândido, Antônio. *Formação da literatura brasileira*. São Paulo: Livraria Martins, 1959.
Carpentier, Alejo. *Literatura y conciencia política en América Latina*. Madrid: Alberto Corazón, 1969.
———. *La novela latinoamericana en vísperas de un nuevo siglo y otros ensayos*. Mexico: Siglo XXI, 1981.
———. *El reino de este mundo*. Santiago, Chile. Editorial ORBE, 1972.
———. *Tientos y diferencias*. 1967; rpt. Buenos Aires: California Editorial, 1976.
Castagnino, Raúl H. *Escritores hispanoamericanos; desde otros ángulos de simpatía*. Buenos Aires: Ed. Nova, 1971.

Chaves, Flávio Loureiro. *Ficção Latino-Americana.* Porto Alegre: Univ. Federal do Rio Grande do Sul, 1973.
Chiampi, Irlemar. *O realismo maravilhoso.* São Paulo: Perspectiva, 1980.
Cohen, John M., ed. *Latin American Writing Today.* Baltimore: Penguin Books, 1967.
Coleman, Alexander. *Cinco maestros.* New York: Harcourt, Brace and World, 1969.
Collazos, Oscar, Julio Cortázar, and Mario Vargas Llosa. *Literatura en la revolución y revolución en la literatura: Polémica.* 1970; "2.ª edición" Mexico: Siglo XXI, 1971.
Congreso Internacional de Literatura Iberoamericana, 16th, *Otros mundos, otros fuegos: fantasía y realismo mágico en Iberoamérica.* Ed. Donald A. Yates. East Lansing: Michigan State Univ. Press, Latin American Studies Center, 1975.
Congreso Latinoamericano de Escritores, *Cuestions y quehaceres literarios en el II Congreso Latinoamericano de escritores.* 3 vols. Mexico: Secretaría de Educación Pública, Subsecretaría de Asuntos Culturales, 1967.
Conte, Rafael. *Lenguaje y violencia.* Madrid: Alborak Estudios, 1972.
Cortázar, Julio. *Rayuela.* 1963; "12.ª edición" Buenos Aires: Editorial Sudamericana, 1970.
Coutinho, Afrânio. *Conceito de literatura brasileira.* Rio de Janeiro: Pallas, 1976.
——. *Introdução à literatura no Brasil.* 1959; rpt. Rio de Janeiro: Ed. Distribuidora de Livros Escolares, 1976.
——. *A literatura no Brasil.* 2d ed. Vols. III-VI. Rio de Janeiro: Editorial Sul Americana, 1969-71.
Coutinho, Carlos Nélson. *Literatura e humanismo.* Rio de Janeiro: Paz e Terra, 1967.
Coutinho, Eduardo F., ed. *A unidade diversa: ensaios sobre a nova literatura hispanoamericana.* Rio de Janeiro: Ânima, 1985.
Cunha, Fausto. *Situações da ficção brasileira.* Rio de Janeiro: Paz e Terra, 1970.
Díaz-Seijas, Pedro. *Deslindes: ensayos sobre literatura hispanoamericana y venezolana.* Caracas: E. Armitano, 1972.
Donoso, José. *Historia personal del "boom."* Barcelona: Anagrama, 1972.
Dorfman, Ariel. *Imaginación y violencia en América.* Santiago, Chile: Ed. Universitaria, 1970.
Fernández Moreno, César, ed. *América Latina en su literatura.* "5.ª edición" Mexico: Siglo XXI, 1978.
Flores, Ángel, ed. *Narrativa hispanoamericana: 1816-1981. Historia y antología.* 8 vols. Mexico: Siglo XXI, 1981-85.
Foster, David William, and Virginia Ramos Foster, eds. *Modern Latin American Literature.* 2 vols. New York: Frederick Ungar, 1975.
Franco, Jean. *An Introduction to Spanish-American Literature.* Cambridge: Cambridge Univ. Press, 1975.
——. *The Modern Culture of Latin America: Society and the Artist.* London: Pall Mall, 1967.
Fuentes, Carlos. *La nueva novela hispanoamericana.* Mexico: Cuadernos de Joaquín Mortiz, 1969.
Galeano, Eduardo. *Las venas abiertas de América Latina.* Buenos Aires: Siglo XXI Argentina, 1976.
Gallagher, D. P. *Modern Latin American Literature.* London: Oxford Univ. Press, 1973.
Garbuglio, José Carlos. *Literatura e realidade brasileira: a tentação e a tentativa.* São Paulo: Conselho Estadual de Cultura, 1970.
García Márquez, Gabriel. *El olor de la guayaba: conversaciones con Plinio Apuleyo Mendoza.* Barcelona: Bruguera, 1982.

García Márquez, Gabriel and Mario Vargas Llosa. *La novela en América Latina: Diálogo.* Lima: Carlos Milla Batres and Universidad Nacional de Ingeniería, 1968.
Gertel, Zunilda. *La novela hispanoamericana contemporánea.* Buenos Aires: Nuevos Esquemas, 1970.
Goic, Cedomil. *Historia de la novela hispanoameriana.* Valparaíso: Ediciones Universitarias, 1972.
Gortari, Carlos. *Literatura hispanoamericana.* Madrid: Doncel, 1971.
Green, J. R. *Contemporary Latin American Literature.* Houston: Univ. of Houston Press, 1973.
Grossmann, Rudolf. *Historia y problemas de la literatura latinoamericana.* Trans. Juan C. Probst. Madrid: Ediciones de la Revista de Occidente, 1972.
Guibert, Rita, ed. *Seven Voices.* Trans. Frances Partridge. New Tork: Knopf, 1973.
Harss, Luis, and Barbara Dohmann. *Into the Mainstream: Conversations with Latin American Writers.* New York: Harper and Row, 1967.
Henríquez Ureña, Pedro. *Las corrientes literarias en la América Hispánica.* 2nd ed. Mexico: Fondo de Cultura Económica, 1954. Translation of *Literary Currents in Hispanic America.* Cambridge: Harvard Univ. Press, 1945; rpt. New York: Russell and Russell, 1963.
Jansen, André. *La novela hispanoamericana actual y sus antecedentes.* Barcelona: Ed. Labor, 1974.
Joset, Jacques. *La littérature hispano-américaine.* Paris: Presses Universitaires de France, 1972.
Jozef, Bella. *O espaço reconquistado: linguagem e criação no romance hispano-americano contemporâneo.* Petrópolis: Vozes, 1974.
———. *História da literatura hispano-americana.* Petrópolis: Vozes, 1971.
Lafforgue, Jorge, ed. *Nueva novela latinoamericana 1.* Buenos Aires: Paidós, 1969.
———. *Nueva novela latinoamericana 2.* Buenos Aires: Paidós, 1972.
Lezama Lima, José. *Esferaimagen.* Barcelona: Tusquets, 1970.
———. *La expresión americana.* La Habana, Instituto Nacional de Cultura / Ministerio de Educación, 1957.
Lima, Luiz Costa. *O fingidor e o censor: no Ancien Régime, no Iluminismo e hoje.* Rio de Janeiro: Forense Universitária, 1988.
Linhares, Temístocles. *Primado do nacional: a problemática das literaturas hispanoamericanas.* São Paulo: Conselho Estadual de Cultura, 1976.
Lorenz, Günter, *Diálogo con América Latina: panorama de una literatura del futuro.* Valparaíso: Ediciones Universitarias, 1972.
Loveluck, Juan. *La novela hispanoamericana.* Santiago, Chile: Editorial Universitaria, 1963.
———. *Novelistas hispanoamerianos de hoy.* Madrid: Taurus, 1976.
Lucas, Fábio. *O caráter social da literatura brasileira.* Rio de Janeiro: Paz e Terra, 1970.
———. *A face visível.* Rio de Janeiro: José Olympio, 1973.
———. *Fronteiras imaginárias: crítica.* Rio de Janeiro: Cátedra, 1971.
MacAdam, Alfred J. *Modern Latin American Narratives: The Dreams of Reason.* Chicago: Univ. of Chicago Press, 1977.
Martín, J. L. *Literatura hispanoamericana contemporánea.* Río Piedras, Puerto Rico: Edil, 1973.
Martins, Wilson. *O Modernismo (1916-1945).* São Paulo: Cultrix, 1965.
Ortega, Julio. *La contemplación y la fiesta: ensayos sobre la nueva novela latinoamericna.* Lima: Editorial Universitaria, 1968.
———. *La contemplación y la fiesta: notas sobre la novela latinoamericana actual.* Caracas: Monte Ávila, 1969.
———, ed. *Convergencias, divergencias, incidencias.* Barcelona: Tusquets, 1973.

Ortiz, Renato. *Cultura brasileira e identidade nacional.* São Paulo: Brasiliense, 1985.
Paz, Octavio. *El laberinto de la soledad.* Mexico: Cuadernos Americanos, 1950.
Pizarro, Ana, ed. *La literatura latinoamericana como proceso.* Buenos Aires: Centro Editor de América Latina, 1985.
Pollmann, Leo. *La "nueva novela" en Francia y en Iberoamérica.* Trans. Julio Linares. Madrid: Gredos, 1971.
Portella, Eduardo. *Literatura e realidade nacional.* 2nd ed. Rio de Janeiro: Tempo Brasileiro, 1971.
Pupo-Walker, Enrique. *La vocación literaria del pensamiento histórico en América.* Madrid: Gredos, 1982.
Queiroz, María José de. *Presença da literatura hispano-americana: ensaios.* Belo Horizonte: Imprensa Publicações, 1971.
Rama, Angel. *A cidade das letras.* Trans. Emir Sader. São Paulo: Brasiliense, 1985.
―――. *Transculturación narrativa en América Latina.* Mexico: Siglo XXI, 1982.
Ríos, Roberto. *La novela y el hombre hispanoamericano: el destino humano en la novela hispanoamericana contemporánea.* Buenos Aires: Nueva Imagen, 1969.
Rodríguez Almodóvar, Antonio. *Lecciones de narrativa hispanoamericana: siglo xx.* Seville: Editorial Católica Española, 1972.
Rodríguez Monegal, Emir. *El arte de narrar.* Caracas: Monte Ávila, 1968.
Sábato, Ernesto. *El escritor y sus fantasmas.* Buenos Aires: Editorial Sudamericana, 1970.
Sánchez, L. A. *Historia comparada de las literaturas americanas.* Vol. IV. Buenos Aires: Losada, 1976.
Santiago, Silviano. *Uma literatura nos trópicos.* São Paulo: Perspectiva, 1978.
―――. *Nas malhas do texto: ensaios.* São Paulo: Companhia das Letras, 1989.
Sanz Villanueva, S., and Carlos J. Barbachano, eds. *Teoría de la novela.* Madrid: Sociedad General Española de Librería, 1976.
Schulman, I. A., et al. *Coloquio sobre la novela hispanoamericana.* Mexico: Tezontle, 1967.
Schwartz, Kessel. *A New History of Spanish American Fiction.* 2 vols. Coral Gables, Fla.: Univ. of Miami Press, 1971.
Schwarz, Roberto. *Que horas são?: ensaios.* São Paulo: Companhia das Letras, 1987.
Silva Brito, Mário da. *História do Modernismo brasileiro I: antecedentes da Semana de Arte Moderna.* São Paulo: Saraiva, 1958.
Todorov, Tzvetan. *La conquête de l'Amérique: la question de l'autre.* Paris: Seuil, 1982.
Torre, Guillermo de. *Claves de la literatura hispanoamericana.* Madrid: Taurus, 1959.
Torres-Rioseco, Arturo. *Nueva historia de la gran literatura iberoamericana.* 3rd ed. Buenos Aires: Emecé, 1960.
Vargas Llosa, Mario. *Contra viento y marea.* Barcelona: Seix Barral, 1983.
Vásquez Amaral, José. *The Contemporary Latin American Narrative.* New York: Las Américas, 1970.
Vidal, Hernán. *Literatura hispanoamericana e ideología liberal: surgimiento y crisis.* Buenos Aires: Hispamérica, 1976.
Xirau, Ramón. *Mito y poesía: ensayos sobre literatura contemporánea de lengua española.* Mexico: Univ. Nacional Autónoma, 1973.
Zea, Leopoldo, ed. *América Latina en sus ideas.* Mexico: Siglo XXI, 1986.
Zum Felde, Alberto. *Índice crítico de la narrativa hispanoamericana.* 2 vols. Mexico: Guaraina, 1954-59.

ARTICLES

Aínsa, Fernando. "Algo más que un cohete-señal." *Mundo Nuevo*, March 1969, pp. 71-74.

BIBLIOGRAPHY

Aínsa, Fernando. "La espiral abierta de la novela latinoamericana." *Thesaurus*, No. 28 (1973), pp. 224-60.

———. "Integración y pseudonimia en la novela latinoamericana contemporánea." *Nueva Narrativa Hispanoamericana*, 5 (1975), 239-49.

Alazraki, Jaime. "Borges and the New Latin-American Novel." *Tri-Quarterly*, No. 25 (1972), pp. 379-98.

Alegría, Fernando, et al. "Literatura y política: relación o incompatibilidad?" *Texto Crítico*, No. 4 (1976), pp. 3-35.

Anderson Imbert, Enrique. "Magical Realism in Spanish-American Fiction." *International Fiction Review*, No. 2 (1975), pp. 1-8.

Benavides, Ricardo F. "Hacia una poética del mito en la nueva narrativa hispanoamericana." *Chasqui*, 2, No. 2 (1973), 5-9.

———. "El héroe en la novela hispanoamericana del siglo xx." *Chasqui*, 5, No. 2 (1976), 46-65.

———. "Sobre el realismo en la narrativa hispanoamericana." *Chasqui*, 6, No. 1 (1977), 5-16.

Benedetti, Mario. "El escritor latinoamericano y la revolución posible." *Casa de las Américas*, No. 79 (1973), pp. 136-44.

Brasil, Assis. "A crise positiva da ficção brasileira." *Revista do Livro*, No. 36 (1969), pp. 89-101.

Campo, Xorge del. "La novela actual de América Latina." *Plural* [Mexico City], No. 59 (1976), pp. 62-69.

Cândido, Antônio. "A literatura brasileira em 1972." *Revista Iberoamericana*, 43 (Jan.-June 1977), 5-16.

———. "Literatura e subdesenvolvimento." *Argumento* [Rio de Janeiro], 1 (Oct. 1973), 6-24.

Castagnino, Raúl. "Algunas cuestiones de sociología literaria frente a la nueva novela hispanoamericana." *Nueva Narrativa Hispanoamericana*, 2, No. 2 (1972), 33-44.

Castro, Rosa. "Con Gabriel García Marquez, Cortázar, Fuentes y Vargas Llosa. Estamos escribiendo la novela del hombre latinoamericano." *Siempre*, No. 288 (1967), pp. vi-vii.

Chaves, Flávio Loureiro. "O Brasil na literatura latino-americana." *O Popular* [Goiânia], 1 January 1978, p. 8.

Correa Camiroaga, José. "La vanguardia y la literatura latinoamericana." *Acta Litteraria Academiae Scientiarum Hungaricae*, 17 (1975), 55-70.

Cortázar, Julio. "The Present State of Fiction in Latin America." Trans. Margery A. Safir. *Books Abroad*, 50 (Summer 1976), 522-32.

Coulthard, G. R. "La enajenación en las letras latinoamericanas." *Mundo Nuevo*, December 1969, pp. 41-44.

Dessau, Adalbert. "La novela latinoamericana como conciencia histórica." *Revista Chilena de Literatura*, No. 4 (1971), 5-15.

Donoso Pareja, Miguel. "Literatura refleja y colonialismo cultural." *Cambio*, No. 2 (1976), pp. 69-73.

Earle, Peter G. "Camino oscuro: la novela hispanoamericana contemporánea." *Cuadernos Americanos*, No. 152 (1967), pp. 204-22.

Foster, David W. "La nueva narrativa vista por la crítica." *Nueva Narrativa Hispanoamericana*, 4 (1974), 227-50.

Franco, Jean. "Modernización, resistencia y violencia: la producción literaria de los años sesenta." *Escritura*, 2 (Jan.-June 1977), 3-20.

García Canclini, Néstor. "Para una teoría de la socialización del arte latinoamericano." *Casa de las Américas*, No. 89 (1975), 99-119.

Gertel, Zunilda. "Tres estructuras fundamentales en la narrativa hispanoamericana actual." *Chasqui*, 2, No. 3 (1973), 5-20.
Giordano, Jaime. "Hacia una definición del realismo en la novela hispanoamericana contemporánea." *Nueva Narrativa Hispanoamericana*, 1, No. 1 (1971), 127-32.
―――. "El nivel de la escritura en la narrativa hispanoamericana contemporánea." *Nueva Narrativa Hispanoamericana*, 4 (1974), 307-44.
Gutiérrez Girardot, Rafael. "Literatura y sociedad en Hispanoamérica." *Cuadernos Hispanoamericanos*, 75 (1986), 579-94.
Gyurko, Lanin A. "Modern Hispanic-American Fiction: Novel of Action and Narrative of Consciousness." *Symposium*, No. 25 (1971), pp. 359-76.
Hamilton, Carlos D. "La novela actual de Hispanoamérica." *Cuadernos Americanos*, No. 187 (1973), pp. 223-51.
Irish, James. "Magical Realism: A Search for Caribbean and Latin American Roots." *Literary Half-Yearly*, 2, No. 2 (1970), 127-39.
Jara-Cuadra, René. "Modos de estructuración mítica de la realidad en la novela hispanoamericana contemporánea." *Ibero*, No. 1 (1974), pp. 131-54.
Jozef, Bella. "O romance brasileiro e o ibero-americano na atualidades." *Minas Gerais, Suplemento Literário* [Belo Horizonte], 17 November 1973, pp. 6-7.
Jutras, Luc. "Forma y estilo en la nueva novela hispanoamericana." *Reflexión*, 2, No. 1 (1972), 125-34.
Kadir, Djelal. "Nostalgia or Nihilism: Pop Art and the New Spanish American Novel." *Journal of Spanish Studies, Twentieth Century*, 2 (1974), 127-35.
Kulin, Katalin. "Planos temporales y estructura de *Cien años de soledad* de G. García Márquez." *Acta Litteraria Academiae Scientiarum Hungaricae*, 11 (1969), 291-314.
Lagmanovich, David. "De la lingüística a la crítica literaria: consecuencias para la nueva narrativa." *Nueva Narrativa Hispanoamericana*, 5 (1975), 229-38.
Leal, Luís. "El realismo mágico en la literatura hispanoamericana." *Cuadernos Americanos*, No. 153 (1967), pp. 230-35.
Levy, Kurt L. "The Contemporary Hispanic American Novel: Its Relevance to Society." *Latin American Literary Review*, 3 (Fall-Winter 1974), 7-21.
Loveluck, Juan. "Una revisión de la novela hispanoamericana." *Atenea*, 43, No. (1966), 139-48.
Lucas, Fábio. "Aspectos da ficção brasileira contemporânea." *Minas Gerais, Suplemento Literário* [Belo Horizonte], 27 October 1973, pp. 6-8.
Marín Morales, J. A. "Siete novelistas hispanoamericanos." *Arbor*, No. 293 (1970), pp. 27-43.
Martins, Wilson. "O romance brasileiro contemporâneo." *Convivência*, No. 4 (1976-77), pp. 3-9.
―――. "Tendências da literatura brasileira contemporânea." *Revista Iberoamericana*, 43 (Jan.-June 1977), 17-27.
Mendizábal, J. C. "*Los funerales de la Mamá Grande* de G. García Márquez. El entierro de una tradición o la resurrección de la esperanza." *Letras de Deusto*, 5 (Jan.-June 1975), 121-34.
Morínigo, Mariano. "Lo político en ciclos narrativos de Hispanoamérica." *Nueva Narrativa Hispanoamericana*, 2, No. 2 (1972), 77-92.
Mullen, Edward J. "Spanish-American 'Vanguardismo': The Aesthetics of Revolt." *Language Quarterly*, 9, Nos. 3-4 (1971), 11-16.
Osorio, Nelson. "Problemas del lenguaje y la realidad en la nueva narrativa hispanoamericana." *Problemas de Literatura: Revista Latinoamericana de Teoría y Crítica Literaria*, 1 (Jan. 1972), 37-42.

Pages Larraya, Antonio. "Tradición y renovación en la novela hispanoamericana." *Mundo Nuevo*, April 1969, pp. 76-82.
Pereda, Rosa M. "Novela latinoamericana: posible caracterización de un proceso." *Camp de l'Arpa*, No. 10 (1974), pp. 14-18.
Pope, Randolph D. "La apertura al futuro: una categoría para el análisis de la novela hispanoamericana contemporánea." *Revista Iberoamericana*, 41 (Jan.-June 1975), 15-28.
Rama, Ángel. "Los procesos de transculturación en la narrativa latinoamericana." *Revista de Literatura Hispanoamericana*, No. 5 (1974), pp. 9-38.
Revueltas, José. "Literatura y liberación en América Latina." *Texto Crítico*, No. 2 (1975), pp. 3-28.
Rodríguez Monegal, Emir. "Una escritura revolucionaria." *Revista Iberoamericana*, 37 (July-Dec. 1971), 497-506.
―――. "Latin American Literature." In *World Literature since 1945. Critical Surveys of the Contemporary Literatures of Europe and the Americas*. Ed. Ivan Ivask and Gero von Wilpert. New York: Frederick Ungar, 1973.
―――. "The New Latin American Novel." *Books Abroad*, 44 (Winter 1970), 45-50.
―――. "The New Novelties." *Encounter*, 25 (September 1965), 97-109.
―――. "Notas sobre (hacia) el Boom." *Plural* [Mexico City], No. 4 (1972), pp. 29-32; No. 6 (1972), pp. 35-37; No. 7 (1972), pp. 13-15; No. 8 (1972), pp. 11-14.
Rosenfeld, Anatol. "Reflexões sobre o romance moderno." In *Texto/contexto: ensaios*. São Paulo: Perspectiva, 1969.
Schwartz, Kessel. "Cervantes and Contemporary Hispanic Fiction." *The Southern Quarterly*, 16 (1977), 39-45.
―――. "Themes, Trends, and Textures: The 1960's and the Spanish American Novel." *Hispania*, 55 (December 1972), 817-31.
Schwarz, Roberto. "Criando o romance brasileiro." *Argumento* [Rio de Janeiro], No. 4 (1974), pp. 19-47.
Theodor, Erwin. "A forma do romance moderno – reflexo de experiências coletivas." *Colóquio*, No. 2 (June 1971), pp. 5-13.
Tomaneck, Tomás. "El mito y el lenguaje en la nueva novela hispanoamericana." *Revue des Langues Romanes*, No. 80 (1972), pp. 283-96.
Torre, Guillermo de. "La originalidad de la literatura hispanoamericana." *Revista de Occidente*, 13 (1967), 191-205.
Trigo, Pedro. "Narrativa de un continente en transformación." *Razón y Fé*, No. 188 (1973), pp. 194-206.
Uscatescu, Jorge. "Alienación y estructura." *Cuadernos Hispanoamericanos*, No. 236 (1969), pp. 406-20.
Valbuena Briones, A. "Una cala en el realismo mágico." *Cuadernos Americanos*, No. 166 (1969), pp. 233-41.
Vargas Llosa, Mario. "En torno a la nueva novela latinoamericana." *Revista de la Facultad de Humanidades* [de la Universidad de Puerto Rico, Río Piedras], No. 1 (September 1972), pp. 129-40.
Wheelock, Carter. "Spanish American Fantasy and the 'Believable, Autonomous World.'" *International Fiction Review*, 1 (1974), 1-8.
Yankas, Lautano. "Valores de la narrativa hispanoamericana actual." *Cuadernos Hispanoamericanos*, No. 236 (1969), pp. 334-79.

WORKS BY AND ABOUT JOÃO GUIMARÃES ROSA

Adonias Filho. "A ficção de Guimarães Rosa." In *Guimarães Rosa*. Lisbon: Instituto Luso.Brasileiro, 1969, pp. 11-22.

———. "Guimarães Rosa." *Jornal do Comércio* [Rio de Janeiro], 1 December 1968, Supl. Dom., p. 2.

———. "Renovação no regionalismo." *Jornal do Comércio* [Rio de Janeiro], 7 June 1964, Supl. Dom., p. 5.

Albergaria, Consuelo. *Bruxo da linguagem no Grande sertão: leitura dos elementos esotéricos presentes na obra de Guimarães Rosa*. Rio de Janeiro: Tempo Brasileiro, 1977.

Almada, Ana Maria. "Testamento literário de *Tutaméia*." *O Diário*. [Belo Horizonte], published in 5 parts, 21 September-20 October, 1968, 2º Cad., p. 3.

Alvarenga, Octávio Mello. "*Grande sertão: veredas*." *Correio da Manhã* [Rio de Janeiro], 10 November 1956, 1º Cad., p. 9.

Andrade, Vera Lúca. "Conceituação de jagunço e jagunçagem em *Grande sertão: veredas*." *Minas Gerais, Suplemento Literário* [Belo Horizonte], 28 May 1977, Supl. Lit., pp. 6-7.

Ángelo, Ivan. "Deus e o Diabo no Grande Sertão." *O Diário* [Belo Horizonte], 26 June 1963.

Arrigucci Jr., Davi. "Guimarães Rosa e Góngora: metáforas." *Achados e perdidos*. São Paulo: Polis, 1979, pp. 131-37.

Arroyo, Leonardo. *A cultura popular em Grande sertão: veredas*. Rio de Janeiro: José Olympio, 1984.

———. "De Quelemém a Riobaldo." *Folha da Tarde* [São Paulo], 21 April 1963.

———. "Riobaldo e Fausto." *Folha da Tarde* [São Paulo], 27 December 1964, 1º Cad., p. 2.

Athayde, Tristão de. "O transrealismo de Guimarães Rosa." *Jornal do Brasil* [Rio de Janeiro], 30 August 1963, 1º Cad., p. 6.

Ávila, Afonso. "A autenticidade em Guimarães Rosa." *O Estado de São Paulo*, 12 January 1957, Supl. Lit., p. 4.

Azevedo Filho, Leodegário A. "O discurso de ficção em Guimarães Rosa." *Colóquio*, 15 (Sept. 1973), 27-33.

Barbosa, Alaor. "Notas sobre o *Grande sertão: veredas*." *Minas Gerais* [Belo Horizonte], 26 August, 2 and 9 September, 1978, Supl. Lit.

Bizzarri, Edoardo. "Guimarães Rosa e Vico: notas sobre uma poética rosiana." *O Estado de São Paulo*, 19 November 1972, Supl. Lit., p. 6.

Bolle, Willi. *Fórmula e fábula: teste de uma gramática narrativa aplicada aos contos de Guimarães Rosa*. São Paulo: Perspectiva, 1973.

Brasil, Francisco de Assis. *Guimarães Rosa*. Rio de Janeiro: Organizações Simões, 1969.

———. "Situação da obra." *O Estado de São Paulo*, 30 November 1968, Supl. Lit., p. 1.

Bruyas, Jean-Paul. "Técnicas, estruturas e visão em *Grande sertão: veredas*." *Revista do Instituto de Estudos Brasileiros* [Universidade de São Paulo], No. 18 (1976), pp. 75-92.

Callado, Antônio. "Guimarães Rosa, o épico do grande sertão." *Visão* [Rio de Janeiro], 29, No. 23 (Dec. 1966), 24-28.

Camacho, Fernando. "Entrevista com João Guimarães Rosa." *Humboldt*, No. 37 (1978), pp. 42-53.

Campos, Augusto de. "Um lance de 'dês' do *Grande sertão*." *Revista do Livro* [Rio de Janeiro], 4, No. 16 (Dec. 1959), 9-27.

Campos, Haroldo de. "A linguagem do Iauaretê." In *Guimarães Rosa em três dimensões*. São Paulo: Conselho Estadual de Cultura, 1970, pp. 71-76.
Cândido, Antônio. "Guimarães Rosa e seu *Grande sertão: veredas*." *Jornal do Brasil* [Rio de Janeiro], 21 November 1967, Cad. B, p. 5.
———. "O homem dos avessos." *Tese e antítese*. São Paulo: Companhia Editora Nacional, 1964, pp. 119-40.
———. "Jagunços mineiros de Cláudio a Guimarães Rosa." In *Vários escritos*. São Paulo: Livraria Duas Cidades, 1970, pp. 133-60.
———. "*Sagarana*." *O Jornal* [Rio de Janeiro], 21 July 1946, pp. 1, 10.
———. "O sertão e o mundo." *Diálogo* [São Paulo], 8 (November 1957), 5-18.
Cannabrava, Euryalo. "Guimarães Rosa e a linguagem literária." *Diário de Notícias* [Rio de Janeiro], 8 April 1956, Supl. Lit., pp. 1, 4.
———. "Técnica literária e técnica lingüística." *Diário de Notícias* [Rio de Janeiro], 2 December 1956, Supl. Lit., pp. 2, 4.
Capovilla, Maurice. "O recado do morro." *Revista do Livro* [Rio de Janeiro], 6, No. 25 (March 1964), 131-43.
Cardoso, Wilton. "A estrutura da composição em Guimarães Rosa." In *Guimarães Rosa*. Belo Horizonte: Centro de Estudos Mineiros, 1966, pp. 31-50.
Castro, Manuel Antônio de. *O homem provisório no Grande Ser-tão: um estudo de Grande sertão: veredas*. Rio de Janeiro: Tempo Brasileiro, 1976.
Castro, Nei Leandro de. *Universo e vocabulário do Grande sertão*. Rio de Janeiro: José Olympio, 1970.
César, Guilhermino. "Com a vida." *Correio do Povo* [Porto Alegre], 14 June 1975, Cad. de Sáb., p. 3.
Chamie, Mário. "Citrodia, Blau e Riobaldo." *O Estado de São Paulo*, 17 October 1964, Supl. Lit., p. 6.
Chaves, Flávio, Loureiro. "Guimarães Rosa e a chave do jogo." In *O brinquedo absurdo*. São Paulo: Livraria Editora Polis, 1978, pp. 77-94.
———. "Perfil de Riobaldo." In *Ficção latino-americana*. Porto Alegre: Universidade Federal do Rio Grande do Sul, 1973, pp. 109-32.
Chiampi Cortez, Irlemar. "Narración y metalenguaje en *Grande sertão: veredas*." *Revista Iberoamericana*, 43 (Jan.-June 1977), 199-224.
Coelho, Nelly Novaes. "A arte narrativa e o espírito lúdico de Guimarães Rosa." *O Estado de São Paulo*, 14 April 1974, Supl. Lit., p. 1.
———, and Ivana Versiani. *Guimarães Rosa: dois estudos*. São Paulo: Edições Quíron, 1975.
Costa, Dalila L. Pereira da. *Duas epopéias das Américas: Moby Dick e Grande sertão: veredas, ou: o problema do mal*. Porto: Lello e Irmão Eds., 1974.
Costa, Dante. "O sentido social de *Corpo de baile*." *Para Todos* [Rio de Janeiro], Nos. 40-41 (Jan. 1958).
Coutinho, Eduardo de Faria. *The Process of Revitalization of the Language and Narrative Structure in the Fiction of João Guimarães Rosa and Julio Cortázar*. Valencia: Albatros Ediciones-Hispanófila, 1980.
———. "Guimarães Rosa e a linguagem literária." *Il Confronto Letterario*, 4, No. 7 (May 1987), pp. 173-83.
———. "Guimarães Rosa e os contrapontos da identidade cultural." In *Actas do 1.º Simpósio Interdisciplinar de Estudos Portugueses: Dimensões da Alteridade nas Culturas de Língua Portuguesa – o Outro*. 2 vols. Lisbon: Universidade Nova de Lisboa, 1987, vol. 2, pp. 383-94.
———. "The Committed Character of Guimarães Rosa's Aesthetic Revolution." *Ideologies & Literature*, 3, No. 2 (Fall 1988), 197-216.
———, ed. *Guimarães Rosa*. Fortuna Crítica, 6. Rio de Janeiro: Civilização Brasileira, 1983.

Covizzi, Lenira Marques. *O insólito em Guimarães Rosa e Borges.* São Paulo: Ática, 1978.
Dacanal, José Hildebrando. "A epopéia Riobaldiana." *Nova narrativa épica no Brasil.* Porto Alegre: Livraria Sulina Editora, 1973, pp. 7-108.
―――. "*Grande sertão: veredas* ou a apologia do imanente." *Correio do Povo* [Porto Alegre], 6 Dec. 1969, Cad. de Sáb., pp. 10-12.
Daniel, Mary L. *João Guimarães Rosa: travessia literária.* Rio de Janeiro: José Olympio, 1968.
Dantas, Paulo. "Entre Fabiano e Riobaldo." *O Estado de São Paulo,* 4 April 1964, Supl. Lit., p. 4.
―――. *Sagarana emotiva: cartas de J. Guimarães Rosa [a] Paulo Dantas.* São Paulo: Duas Cidades, 1975.
―――. "Variações sobre o tema: Guimarães Rosa." *Diálogo* [São Paulo], 8 (Nov. 1957), 65-70.
Dias, Fernando Correia. "Aspectos sociológicos de *Grande sertão: veredas.*" In *Guimarães Rosa.* Belo Horizonte: Centro de Estudos Mineiros, 1966, pp. 77-100.
Domingo, Javier. "João Guimarães Rosa y la alegría." *Revista do Livro* [Rio de Janeiro], 5, No. 17 (March 1960), 59-64.
Dourado, W. Autran. "Guimarães Rosa, barroco e coloquial." *Poética de romance: matéria de carpintaria.* São Paulo: Difel, 1976, pp. 36-40.
Doyle, Plínio. "Contribuição à bibliografia de & sobre João Guimarães Rosa." In *Em memória de João Guimarães Rosa.* Rio de Janeiro: José Olympio, 1968.
Duarte, Lélia Maria Parreira. "Riobaldo, personagem tensão." *Minas Gerais* [Belo Horizonte], 14 August 1976, Supl. Lit., pp. 6-7.
Em memória de João Guimarães Rosa. Rio de Janeiro: José Olympio. 1968.
Facó, Aglaêda. *Guimarães Rosa: do ícone ao símbolo. Ensaios de estilística.* Rio de Janeiro: José Olympio, 1982.
Faus, Francesc. "João Guimarães Rosa, le contemplatif transparent." *La Table Ronde,* 195 (1964), 61-70.
Fell, Claude. "Morreu o romancista Guimarães Rosa." Trans. Jean Jacques Villard. *Jornal do Comércio* [Rio de Janeiro], 7 Jan., 1968, Supl. Dom., p. 2.
Ferreira, João. "A obra literária de João Guimarães Rosa e a metafísica." *Correio Brasiliense* [Brasília], 12 November 1971, 3º Cad., p. 3.
Flusser, Vilém. "Guimarães Rosa e a geografia." *Comentário* [Rio de Janeiro], 10, No. 3 (July-Sept. 1969), 39.
Franco, Afonso Arinos de Melo. "O verbo e o logos." Discurso de recepção de Guimarães Rosa na Academia Brasileira de Letras. In *Em memória de João Guimarães Rosa.* Rio de Janeiro: José Olympio, 1968, pp. 89-106.
Freixieiro, Fábio. "Guimarães Rosa em face de conceitos lingüísticos modernos: ensaios rosianos, outros ensaios e documentos." In *Da razão à emoção II.* Rio de Janeiro: Tempo Brasileiro, 1971, pp. 136-43.
Galvão, Walnice Nogueira. *As formas do falso.* São Paulo: Perspectiva, 1972.
―――. *Mitológica rosiana.* São Paulo: Ática, 1978.
Garbuglio, José Carlos. "Guimarães Rosa: a gênese de uma obra." *Revista Iberoamericana,* 43 (Jan.-June 1977), 183-98.
―――. "O fato épico e outros fatos." *O Estado de São Paulo,* 25 November 1967, Supl. Lit., p. 4.
―――. *O mundo movente de Guimarães Rosa.* São Paulo: Ática, 1972.
Gersen, Bernardo. "Regionalismo e universalismo em Guimarães Rosa." *Diário de Notícias* [Rio de Janeiro], 6 May 1956, Supl. Lit., pp. 1, 4.
―――. "Veredas no *Grande sertão.*" *O Estado de São Paulo,* 24 March 1962, Supl. Lit., p. 6.

Grünewald, José Lino. "Rosa da prosa." *Correio da Manhã* [Rio de Janeiro], 21 November 1967, 2º Cad., p. 1.
Guimarães, Vicente. *Joãozito: infância de Guimarães Rosa*. Rio de Janeiro: José Olympio, 1972.
Hansen, João Adolfo. "Terceira margem." *Folha de São Paulo*, 20 Nov. 1987, Folhetim, pp. 2-5.
Hoisel, Evelina de C. de Sá. "Elementos dramáticos da estrutura de *Grande sertão: veredas*." *Minas Gerais* [Belo Horizonte], 29 January 1977, Supl. Lit., pp. 6-8.
Houaiss, Antônio. "Entrevista." *José*, Nos. 5-6 (Nov.-Dec. 1976), pp. 18-31.
Jozef, Bella. "Guimarães Rosa e a literatura hispano-americana." *Jornal do Comércio* [Rio de Janeiro], 3 and 10 December 1967, Supl. Dom., p. 3.
Krähenbühl, Olívia. "A linguagem como tema." *Diálogo* [São Paulo], 8 (Nov. 1957), 43-44.
Lacerda, Virgínia Cortes de. "Guimarães Rosa e a ficção moderna *(Grande sertão: veredas)*." *Leitores e Livros* [Rio de Janeiro], 9, No. 35 (1959), 129-49.
Leite, Dante Moreira. "A ficção de Guimarães Rosa." *O Estado de São Paulo*, 24 and 31 August 1963, 7 and 14 September 1963, Supl. Lit.
———. "*Grande sertão: veredas*." *O Estado de São Paulo*, 15 and 22 July 1961, Supl. Lit., p. 3.
Lima Filho, Luís Costa. "A expressão orgânica de um escritor moderno." *Diálogo* [São Paulo], 8 (Nov. 1957), 71-90.
———. "Mito e provérbio em Guimarães Rosa." In *A metamorfose do silêncio*. Rio de Janeiro: Editora Eldorado, 1974, pp. 49-66.
———. "O mundo em perspectiva: Guimarães Rosa." *Tempo Brasileiro*, No. 6 (1963), pp. 67-83.
———. "O sertão e o mundo." In *Porque literatura*. Petrópolis: Vozes, 1966, pp. 73-99.
Lisboa, Henriqueta. "A poesia de *Grande sertão: veredas*." *Revista do Livro* [Rio de Janeiro], 3, No. 12 (Dec. 1958), 141-46.
———. "O motivo infantil na obra de Guimarães Rosa." In *Guimarães Rosa*. Belo Horizonte: Centro de Estudos Mineiros, 1966, pp. 11-16.
Lopes, Óscar. "Guimarães Rosa." *Seara Nova* [Lisbon], No. 1425 (July 1964).
———. "Guimarães Rosa – intenções de um estilo." In *Guimarães Rosa*. Lisbon: Instituto Luso-Brasileiro, 1969, pp. 23-40.
Lorenz, Günter W. "Diálogo con Guimarães Rosa." *Mundo Nuevo*, March 1970, pp. 27-47. Later included in Lorenz, *Diálogo con América Latina*, q.v.
———. "Um mundo em estado virgem." Trans. Helma Blöhm. *Correio da Manhã* [Rio de Janeiro], 7 November 1964, 2º Cad., p. 2.
Lowe, Elizabeth. "Dialogues of *Grande sertão: veredas*." *Luso-Brazilian Review*, 13 (Winter 1976), 231-43.
Lucas, Fábio. "Personagens de ficção." *O Estado de São Paulo*, 19 October 1957, Supl. Lit., p. 4.
Machado, Ana Maria. *Recado do nome: leitura de Guimarães Rosa à luz do nome de seus personagens*. Rio de Janeiro: Imago, 1976.
Marques, Oswaldino. "Canto e plumagem das palavras." In *Ensaios escolhidos*. Rio de Janeiro: Civilização Brasileira, 1968, pp. 77-148.
Martins, Heitor. *Do barroco a Guimarães Rosa*. Belo Horizonte: Ed. Itatiaia, 1983.
Martins, Wilson. "Jõe Guimarró." *O Estado de São Paulo*, 8 May 1965, Supl. Lit., p. 2.
———. "Literaturnost." *O Estado de São Paulo*, 13 January 1968, Supl. Lit., p. 4.
———. "Um novo regionalismo: Guimarães Rosa." *Humboldt*, 5, No. 12 (1965), 26-27.

Martins, Wilson. "Structural Perspectivism in Guimarães Rosa." In *The Brazilian Novel*. Ed. Heitor Martins. Bloomington: Indiana University Press, 1976.

Mendonça, Fernando. "Guimarães Rosa e Aquilino." *O Estado de São Paulo*, 5 October 1963, Supl. Lit., p. 1.

Meyer-Clason, Curt. "Guimarães Rosa e a língua alemã." In *Guimarães Rosa*. Lisbon: Instituto Luso-Brasileiro, 1969, pp. 41-59.

———. "A tradução ou o encontro procurado." *Revista do Instituto de Estudos Brasileiros* [Universidade de São Paulo], 1 (1966), 139-56.

Milliet, Sérgio. "*Grande sertão: veredas.*" *O Estado de São Paulo*, 31 July 1956, Supl. Lit., p. 8.

Miranda, Wander Melo. "O espaço do sertão em *Grande sertão: veredas*." *Minas Gerais* [Belo Horizonte], 19 August 1978, Supl. Lit., pp. 6-7.

Monteiro, Adolfo Casais. "O erudito e o popular em *Grande sertão: veredas*." *O Estado de São Paulo*, 1 March 1958, Supl. Lit., p. 6.

———. "Guimarães Rosa não é escritor regionalista." *O Estado de São Paulo*, 8 March 1958, Supl. Lit., p. 3.

Montenegro, Braga. "Guimarães Rosa, novelista." *Minas Gerais* [Belo Horizonte], 6 July 1968, Supl. Lit., pp. 2-3.

Montenegro, Olívio. "Fala e linguagem." *O Jornal* [Rio de Janeiro], 23 September 1956, pp. 1, 4.

Mourão, Rui. "João Guimarães Rosa — *Grande sertão: veredas*." *Tendência*, August 1957, pp. 84-86.

———. "Processo da linguagem, processo do homem." *O Estado de São Paulo*, 2 August 1969, Supl. Lit., p. 5.

Nascimento, Edna Maria F. S. & Lenira Marques Covizzi. *João Guimarães Rosa: homem plural, escritor singular*. Lendo. São Paulo: Atual, 1988.

Nazareth, Luiz Fernando. "O barroco no *Grande sertão*." *Diário Carioca* [Rio de Janeiro], 8 March 1959, 2ª sec., p. 3.

Novis, Vera. "Iniciação a *Tutaméia*." *Folha de São Paulo*, 20 Nov. 1987, Folhetim, pp. 8-10.

Nunes, Benedito. "Guimarães Rosa." In *O dorso do tigre*. São Paulo: Perspectiva, 1969, pp. 143-212.

———. "A Rosa o que é de Rosa." *O Estado de São Paulo*, 22 March 1969, Supl. Lit., p. 1.

Oliveira, Franklin de. "A egrégia fidelidade." *Correio da Manhã* [Rio de Janeiro], 8 December 1968, 4.º Cad., p. 3.

———. "Guimarães Rosa." In *A literatura no Brasil*. Ed. Afrânio Coutinho. 2nd ed. V: Modernismo. Rio de Janeiro: Editorial Sul Americana, 1970, pp. 402-48.

Paiva, José Rodrigues de. "As surpresas do mágico." In *As surpresas do mágico e outros ensaios*. Recife: Encontro, 1985.

Pérez, Renard. "Guimarães Rosa." *Revista de Cultura Brasileña*, 6 (June 1967), 101-06.

Pimentel, Osmar. "O sertanejo no mundo." *Folha da Manhã* [São Paulo], 18 November 1956, 6º Cad., p. 2.

Pires, Herculano. "Guimarães Rosa, o Demiurgo." *Diário da Noite* [São Paulo], 7 April 1956.

———. "Um livro que derruba a barreira entre língua literária e falada." *Diário da Noite* [São Paulo], 30 March 1957.

Pires Filho, Ormindo. "Um déficit sociológico em Guimarães Rosa?" *Diário de Pernambuco* [Recife], 4 July 1976, 4º Cad., p. 4.

Pontes, Joel. "O geralista Riobaldo." *O Jornal* [Rio de Janeiro], 24 February 1957, 3ª sec., p. 2.

Portella, Eduardo. "A estória cont(r)a a história." *Jornal do Brasil* [Rio de Janeiro], 30 December 1967, Cad. B, p. 3.
———. "Um romance e sua dialética." *Jornal do Comérco* [Rio de Janeiro], 4 August 1957, 3º Cad., p. 10.
———. "Um romance síntese." *Correio da Manhã* [Rio de Janeiro], 1 December 1956, 1º Cad., p. 10.
Prada, Cecília. "Três depoimentos sobre Guimarães Rosa." *Jornal do Brasil* [Rio de Janeiro], 3 August 1958, 1º Cad., p. 5.
Proença, M. Cavalcânti. *Trilhas no Grande sertão*. Rio de Janeiro: Ministério da Educação e Cultura, 1958.
Ramos, Maria Luísa. "O elemento poético em *Grande sertão: veredas*." In *Guimarães Rosa*. Belo Horizonte: Centro de Estudos Mineiros, 1966, pp. 51-76.
———. "O mundo mítico do sertão de Rosa." *Minas Gerais* [Belo Horizonte], 9 October 1971, Supl. Lit., p. 7.
Ribeiro, Léo Gilson. "O sertão rude de Guimarães Rosa." *O Estado de São Paulo*, 15 October 1966, Jornal da Tarde, p. 5.
Riedel, Dirce Cortes. "O conflito da experiência humana na linguagem metafórica." *Jornal do Comércio* [Rio de Janeiro], 31 May, 1964.
Rodríguez Monegal, Emir. "En busca de Guimarães Rosa." *Mundo Nuevo*, February 1968, pp. 4-24.
Rónai, Paulo, ed. *Seleta de João Guimarães Rosa*. Rio de Janeiro: José Olympio, 1973.
———. "Três motivos em *Grande sertão: veredas*." *Diário de Notícias* [Rio de Janeiro], 16 December 1956, Supl. Lit., p. 2.
Rosa, João Guimarães. *Ave, palavra*. Rio de Janeiro: José Olympio, 1970.
———. *Estas estórias*. Rio de Janeiro: José Olympio, 1969.
———. *Grande sertão: veredas*. 2nd ed. ["Texto definitivo"]. Rio de Janeiro: José Olympio, 1958.
———. *Manuelzão e Miguilim*. Rio de Janeiro: José Olympio, 1970.
———. *Noites do sertão*. Rio de Janeiro: José Olympio, 1965.
———. *No Urubùquaquá, no Pinhém*. Rio de Janeiro: José Olympio, 1965.
———. *Primeiras estórias*. Rio de Janeiro: José Olympio, 1962.
———. *Sagarana*. Rio de Janeiro: Editora Universal, 1946.
———. *Tutaméia*. Rio de Janeiro: José Olympio, 1967.
———. "O verbo e o logos – discurso de posse na Academia Brasileira de Letras." In *Em memória de João Guimarães Rosa*. Rio de Janeiro: José Olympio, 1968.
———, and Edoardo Bizarri. *Correspondência com o tradutor italiano*. São Paulo: Instituto Cultural Italo-Brasileiro, 1972.
Rosa, Vilma Guimarães. *Relembramentos: João Guimarães Rosa, meu pai*. Rio de Janeiro: Nova Fronteira, 1983.
Sáfady, Naief. "Sertão e expressão." *O Estado de São Paulo*, 26 September 1964, Supl. Lit., p. 4.
Sales, Fritz Teixeira de. "O 'caso' Guimarães Rosa." *O Estado de Minas* [Belo Horizonte], 28 April 1976, 2ª sec., p. 6.
Santos, Júlia Conceição Fonseca. *Nomes dos personagens em Guimarães Rosa*. Rio de Janeiro: Instituto Nacional do Livro, 1971.
Schüler, Donaldo. "Significante e significado em *Grande sertão: veredas*." *Correio do Povo* [Porto Alegre], 23 and 30 May 1965, 1º Cad., pp. 12, 23.
———. "O racional e o irracional no monólogo de Riobaldo." *Correio do Povo* [Porto Alegre], 30 December 1963, Cad. de Sáb.
Schwarz, Roberto. "*Grande sertão*: a fala." In *A sereia e o desconfiado: ensaios críticos*. Rio de Janeiro: Civilização Brasileira, 1965, pp. 23-27.

Schwartz, Roberto. "*Grande sertão* e *Dr. Faustus.*" In *A sereia e o desconfiado: ensaios críticos* Rio de Janeiro: Civilização Brasileira, 1965, pp. 28-36.
Silva, Dora Ferreira da. "O demoníaco em *Grande sertão: veredas.*" *Diálogo* [São Paulo], 8 (Nov. 1957), 29-34.
Silva, Vítor Emanuel de Aguiar e. "Visão do mundo e estilo em *Grande sertão: veredas.*" In *Guimarães Rosa*. Lisbon: Instituto Luso-Brasileiro, 1969, pp. 61-79.
Simões, Roberto. "Notícia da visitação nas veredas do *Grande sertão.*" *Diálogo* [São Paulo], 8 (Nov. 1957), 45-64.
Souza, Ronaldes de Melo e. *Ficção e realidade: diálogo e catarse em "Grande sertão: veredas."* Brasília: Clube de Poesia, 1978.
―――. "Travessia e epifania em *Grande sertão: veredas.*" *Cultura*, 15 (1974), 111-23.
―――. "O valor poético-metafísico da obra de Guimarães Rosa." *Minas Gerais* [Belo Horizonte], 20 May 1978, Supl. Lit., pp. 6-7.
Sperber, Suzi Frankl. *Caos e cosmos: leituras de Guimarães Rosa*. São Paulo: Duas Cidades, 1976.
―――. *Guimarães Rosa: signo e sentimento*. São Paulo: Ática, 1982.
Theodor, Erwin. "Deformação como elemento constitutivo em Guimarães Rosa e Martin Walser." *O Estado de São Paulo*, 20 and 27 April 1968, Supl. Lit.
Vargas, Milton. "Visão e descrição." *Diálogo* [Sãu Paulo], 8 (Nov. 1957), 19-28.
Vargas Llosa, Mario. "Epopéia do sertão, torre de Babel ou manual de Satanismo?" Trans. L. C. A. [Luis Correia de Araújo?], *Minas Gerais* [Belo Horizonte], 29 November 1969, Supl. Lit., p. 2; rpt. from *Amaru*, No. 2 (1967), pp. 70-72.
Ventura, Aglaêda Facó. "Linguística e literatura – *Grande sertão: veredas.*" *Correio Brasiliense* [Brasília], 15 June 1975, 2º Cad., p. 5.
Viggiano, Alan. *Itinerário de Riobaldo Tatarana*. Rio de Janeiro: José Olympio, 1978.
Vizioli, Paulo. "Guimarães Rosa e William Faulkner." *O Estado de São Paulo*, 11 April 1970, Supl. Lit., p. 1.
Ward, Teresinha. *O discurso oral em Grande sertão: veredas*. São Paulo: Duas Cidades, 1984.
Xisto, Pedro. "À busca da poesia." In *Guimarães Rosa em três dimensões*. São Paulo: Conselho Estadual de Cultura, 1970, pp. 7-39.

NORTH CAROLINA STUDIES IN THE ROMANCE LANGUAGES AND LITERATURES

I.S.B.N. Prefix 0-8078-

Recent Titles

RICHARD SANS PEUR, EDITED FROM "LE ROMANT DE RICHART" AND FROM GILLES CORROZET'S "RICHART SANS PAOUR", by Denis Joseph Conlon. 1977. (No. 192). *-9192-4.*
MARCEL PROUST'S GRASSET PROOFS. *Commentary and Variants,* by Douglas Alden. 1978. (No. 193). *-9193-2.*
MONTAIGNE AND FEMINISM, by Cecile Insdorf. 1977. (No. 194). *-9194-0.*
SANTIAGO F. PUGLIA, AN EARLY PHILADELPHIA PROPAGANDIST FOR SPANISH AMERICAN INDEPENDENCE, by Merle S. Simmons. 1977. (No. 195). *-9195-9.*
BAROQUE FICTION-MAKING. A STUDY OF GOMBERVILLE'S "POLEXANDRE", by Edward Baron Turk. 1978. (No. 196). *-9196-7.*
THE TRAGIC FALL: DON ÁLVARO DE LUNA AND OTHER FAVORITES IN SPANISH GOLDEN AGE DRAMA, by Raymond R. MacCurdy. 1978. (No. 197). *-9197-5.*
A BAHIAN HERITAGE. An Ethnolinguistic Study of African Influences on Bahian Portuguese, by William W. Megenney. 1978. (No. 198). *-9198-3.*
"LA QUERELLE DE LA ROSE": Letters and Documents, by Joseph L. Baird and John R. Kane. 1978. (No. 199). *-9199-1.*
TWO AGAINST TIME. *A Study of the Very Present Worlds of Paul Claudel and Charles Péguy,* by Joy Nachod Humes. 1978. (No. 200). *-9200-9.*
TECHNIQUES OF IRONY IN ANATOLE FRANCE. Essay on *Les Sept Femmes de la Barbe-Bleue,* by Diane Wolfe Levy. 1978. (No. 201). *-9201-7.*
THE PERIPHRASTIC FUTURES FORMED BY THE ROMANCE REFLEXES OF "VADO (AD)" PLUS INFINITIVE, by James Joseph Champion. 1978. (No. 202). *-9202-5.*
THE EVOLUTION OF THE LATIN /b/-/ɥ/ MERGER: A Quantitative and Comparative Analysis of the *B-V* Alternation in Latin Inscriptions, by Joseph Louis Barbarino. 1978. (No. 203). *-9203-3.*
METAPHORIC NARRATION: THE STRUCTURE AND FUNCTION OF METAPHORS IN "A LA RECHERCHE DU TEMPS PERDU", by Inge Karalus Crosman. 1978. (No. 204). *-9204-1.*
LE VAIN SIECLE GUERPIR. A Literary Approach to Sainthood through Old French Hagiography of the Twelfth Century, by Phyllis Johnson and Brigitte Cazelles. 1979. (No. 205). *-9205-X.*
THE POETRY OF CHANGE: A STUDY OF THE SURREALIST WORKS OF BENJAMIN PÉRET, by Julia Field Costich. 1979. (No. 206). *-9206-8.*
NARRATIVE PERSPECTIVE IN THE POST-CIVIL WAR NOVELS OF FRANCISCO AYALA "MUERTES DE PERRO" AND "EL FONDO DEL VASO", by Maryellen Bieder. 1979. (No. 207). *-9207-6.*
RABELAIS: HOMO LOGOS, by Alice Fiola Berry. 1979. (No. 208). *-9208-4.*
"DUEÑAS" AND "DONCELLAS": A STUDY OF THE "DOÑA RODRÍGUEZ" EPISODE IN "DON QUIJOTE", by Conchita Herdman Marianella. 1979. (No. 209). *-9209-2.*
PIERRE BOAISTUAU'S "HISTOIRES TRAGIQUES": A STUDY OF NARRATIVE FORM AND TRAGIC VISION, by Richard A. Carr. 1979. (No. 210). *-9210-6.*
REALITY AND EXPRESSION IN THE POETRY OF CARLOS PELLICER, by George Melnykovich. 1979. (No. 211). *-9211-4.*
MEDIEVAL MAN, HIS UNDERSTANDING OF HIMSELF, HIS SOCIETY, AND THE WORLD, by Urban T. Holmes, Jr. 1980. (No. 212). *-9212-2.*
MÉMOIRES SUR LA LIBRAIRIE ET SUR LA LIBERTÉ DE LA PRESSE, introduction and notes by Graham E. Rodmell. 1979. (No. 213). *-9213-0.*
THE FICTIONS OF THE SELF. THE EARLY WORKS OF MAURICE BARRES, by Gordon Shenton. 1979. (No. 214). *-9214-9.*

When ordering please cite the *ISBN Prefix* plus the last four digits for each title.

Send orders to: University of North Carolina Press
P.O. Box 2288
CB# 6215
Chapel Hill, NC 27515-2288
U.S.A.

NORTH CAROLINA STUDIES IN THE ROMANCE LANGUAGES AND LITERATURES

I.S.B.N. Prefix 0-8078-

Recent Titles

CECCO ANGIOLIERI. A STUDY, by Gifford P. Orwen. 1979. (No. 215). *-9215-7.*
THE INSTRUCTIONS OF SAINT LOUIS: A CRITICAL TEXT, by David O'Connell. 1979. (No. 216). *-9216-5.*
ARTFUL ELOQUENCE, JEAN LEMAIRE DE BELGES AND THE RHETORICAL TRADITION, by Michael F. O. Jenkins. 1980. (No. 217). *-9217-3.*
A CONCORDANCE TO MARIVAUX'S COMEDIES IN PROSE, edited by Donald C. Spinelli. 1979. (No. 218). 4 volumes, *-9218-1* (set); *-9219-X* (v. 1); *-9220-3* (v. 2); *-9221-1* (v. 3); *-9222-X* (v. 4).
ABYSMAL GAMES IN THE NOVELS OF SAMUEL BECKETT, by Angela B. Moorjani. 1982. (No. 219). *-9223-8.*
GERMAIN NOUVEAU DIT HUMILIS: ÉTUDE BIOGRAPHIQUE, par Alexandre L. Amprimoz. 1983. (No. 220). *-9224-6.*
THE "VIE DE SAINT ALEXIS" IN THE TWELFTH AND THIRTEENTH CENTURIES: AN EDITION AND COMMENTARY, by Alison Goddard Elliot. 1983. (No. 221). *-9225-4.*
THE BROKEN ANGEL: MYTH AND METHOD IN VALÉRY, by Ursula Franklin. 1984. (No. 222). *-9226-2.*
READING VOLTAIRE'S "CONTES": A SEMIOTICS OF PHILOSOPHICAL NARRATION, by Carol Sherman. 1985. (No. 223). *-9227-0.*
THE STATUS OF THE READING SUBJECT IN THE "LIBRO DE BUEN AMOR", by Marina Scordilis Brownlee. 1985. (No. 224). *-9228-9.*
MARTORELL'S "TIRANT LO BLANCH": A PROGRAM FOR MILITARY AND SOCIAL REFORM IN FIFTEENTH-CENTURY CHRISTENDOM, by Edward T. Aylward. 1985. (No. 225). *-9229-7.*
NOVEL LIVES: THE FICTIONAL AUTOBIOGRAPHIES OF GUILLERMO CABRERA INFANTE AND MARIO VARGAS LLOSA, by Rosemary Geisdorfer Feal. 1986. (No. 226). *-9230-0.*
SOCIAL REALISM IN THE ARGENTINE NARRATIVE, by David William Foster. 1986. (No. 227). *-9231-9.*
HALF-TOLD TALES: DILEMMAS OF MEANING IN THREE FRENCH NOVELS, by Philip Stewart. 1987. (No. 228). *-9232-7.*
POLITIQUES DE L'ECRITURE BATAILLE/DERRIDA: le sens du sacré dans la pensée française du surréalisme à nos jours, par Jean-Michel Heimonet. 1987. (No. 229). *-9233-5.*
GOD, THE QUEST, THE HERO: THEMATIC STRUCTURES IN BECKETT'S FICTION, by Laura Barge. 1988. (No. 230). *-9235-1.*
THE NAME GAME. WRITING/FADING WRITER IN "DE DONDE SON LOS CANTANTES", by Oscar Montero. 1988. (No. 231). *-9236-X.*
GIL VICENTE AND THE DEVELOPMENT OF THE COMEDIA, by René Pedro Garay. 1988. (No. 232). *-9234-3.*
HACIA UNA POÉTICA DEL RELATO DIDÁCTICO: OCHO ESTUDIOS SOBRE "EL CONDE LUCANOR", por Aníbal A. Biglieri. 1989. (No. 233). *-9237-8.*
A POETICS OF ART CRITICISM: THE CASE OF BAUDELAIRE, by Timothy Raser. 1989. (No. 234). *-9238-6.*
UMA CONCORDÀNCIA DO ROMANCE "GRANDE SERTÃO: VEREDAS" DE JOÃO GUIMARÃES ROSA, by Myriam Ramsey and Paul Dixon. 1989. (No. 235). Microfiche, *-9239-4.*
CYCLOPEAN SONG: MELANCHOLY AND AESTHETICISM IN GÓNGORA'S "FÁBULA DE POLIFEMO Y GALATEA", by Kathleen Hunt Dolan. 1990. (No. 236). *-9240-8.*
THE "SYNTHESIS" NOVEL IN LATIN AMERICA. A STUDY ON JOÃO GUIMARÃES ROSA'S "GRANDE SERTÃO: VEREDAS", by Eduardo de Faria Coutinho. 1991. (No. 237). *-9241-6.*

When ordering please cite the *ISBN Prefix* plus the last four digits for each title.

Send orders to: University of North Carolina Press
P.O. Box 2288
CB# 6215
Chapel Hill, NC 27515-2288
U.S.A.

The Department of Romance Studies Digital Arts and Collaboration Lab at the University of North Carolina at Chapel Hill is proud to support the digitization of the North Carolina Studies in the Romance Languages and Literatures series.

DEPARTMENT OF Romance Studies

Digital Arts and Collaboration Lab

www.ingramcontent.com/pod-product-compliance
Lightning Source LLC
Chambersburg PA
CBHW020416230426
43663CB00007BA/1196